CHANGING MIGRATION PATTERNS WITHIN THE UNITED STATES

Curtis C. Roseman
University of Illinois

RESOURCE PAPERS FOR COLLEGE GEOGRAPHY NO. 77-2

Copyright 1977
by the
Association of American Geographers
1710 Sixteenth Street, N.W.
Washington, D.C. 20009

Library of Congress Card Number 76-57033
ISBN 0-89291-123-9

FOREWORD

In 1968, the Commission on College Geography of the Association of American Geographers published its first Resource Paper, *Theories of Urban Location,* by Brian J. L. Berry. In 1974, coinciding with the termination of NSF funding for the Commission, Resource Paper number 28 appeared, *The Underdevelopment and Modernization of the Third World,* by Anthony R. deSouza and Philip W. Porter. Of the many CCG activities, the Resource Papers Series became an effective means for permitting both teachers and students to keep abreast of developments in the field.

Because of the popularity and usefulness of the Resource Papers, the AAG applied for and received a two-year grant from NSF to continue to produce Resource Papers and to put the series on a self-supporting basis. The 1977 Series is the first group produced entirely with AAG funding.

In an effort to increase the utility of these papers, the Resource Papers Panel has attempted to be particularly sensitive to the currency of materials for undergraduate geography courses and to the writing style of these papers. The present Panel continues to affirm the original purposes of the Series, which are quoted below:

> The Resource Papers have been developed as expository documents for the use of both the student and the instructor. They are experimental in that they are designed to supplement existing texts and to fill a gap between significant research in American geography and readily accessible materials. The papers are concerned with important concepts or topics in modern geography and focus on one of three general themes: geographic theory; policy implications; or contemporary social relevance. They are designed to complement a variety of undergraduate college geography courses at the introductory and advanced level.

The Resource Papers are developed, printed, and distributed under the auspices of the Association of American Geographers. The ideas presented in these papers do not imply endorsement by the AAG.

Many individuals have assisted in producing these Resource Papers, and we wish to acknowledge those who assisted the Panel in reviewing the authors' prospectuses, in reading and commenting on the various drafts, and in making helpful suggestions. The Panel also acknowledges the perceptive suggestions and editorial assistance of Jane F. Castner of the AAG Central Office.

Salvatore J. Natoli
Educational Affairs Director
Association of American Geographers
Project Director and Editor, Resource Papers Series

Resource Papers Panel:

John F. Lounsbury, Arizona State University
Mark S. Monmonier, Syracuse University
Harold A. Winters, Michigan State University

PREFACE

Recently, dramatic changes have occurred in the patterns of population distribution within the United States. These have resulted largely from changes in migration behavior. People are making migration decisions which are quite different from those made before the middle 1960's, often choosing types of destinations that have not been growing since before the turn of the century. Previous migration patterns, which were fairly consistent for several decades, included movements from smaller to larger urban centers and significant movement from rural to urban areas. Now there is a tendency toward movements down the size hierarchy of urban centers and movements from urban areas to rural areas (principally rural areas near metropolitan centers, but also a surprising number of isolated rural areas and small towns). Similar patterns have been observed in other developed nations.

This Resource Paper will acquaint the student with the rapidly emerging migration patterns in the United States. We want to know about recent migration decisions that are, and will be, affecting the overall distribution of population. The new migration patterns will be contrasted to older ones to develop an appreciation for the recent changes in locational decisions. Ideas of migration theory, especially those relating to decision-making, will be presented so that the student can fully appreciate the fundamental mechanisms underlying the patterns that can be described by maps. This approach is used so that we may speculate on migration trends in the near future, not just through simple extrapolation of current patterns, but by predictions based on generalizations which may have longer-term validity.

I would like to acknowledge the following persons for contributing to this work by their critiques of early drafts of the manuscript and/or allowing me to borrow their ideas: Fred M. Shelley, Sallie M. Ives, Richard E. Groop, Elizabeth Mercer Roseman, Edward V. Karl, Francis Simbo, and John Muhr. Helpful reviews received from Richard L. Morrill, Lawrence A. Brown, and Wilbur Zelinsky were also much appreciated. Finally, I thank James A. Bier for his cartographic work and Darlene L. Bennett for typing the manuscript.

Curtis C. Roseman
University of Illinois
March 1977

SUGGESTIONS FOR CLASS USE

This Resource Paper can be used in conjunction with any course that deals with population distribution, migration patterns, or migration processes. Basic ideas of migration theory are introduced in a straightforward manner and are tied to the migration patterns that can be observed on maps (which are used extensively in the paper). This, along with appropriate references to the literature, will enable the instructor and student to extend discussions to a variety of issues that are linked to migration. In addition, the paper introduces some data sources and some techniques of data gathering, organization, and analysis so that the student may apply many of the ideas in actual empirical work. In sum, the student is provided with the foundation—theoretical, factual, and methodological—to be challenged to think about future population movement, changing population distribution, and their implications.

CONTENTS

PREFACE iv

SUGGESTIONS FOR CLASS USE v

I. THE STUDY OF MIGRATION 1

II. MIGRATION AS A COMPONENT OF POPULATION CHANGE... 1

    Demographic Equation 1

    Natural and Migrational Population Change.. 2

    Predicting Components of Population Change.. 3

    The Lowry Hypothesis... 3

III. MIGRATION DECISION-MAKING 4

    The Decision: To Move 5

    The Decision: Where to Move... 6

    Long-Term Place Preferences... 6

    Search Spaces 7

    Choosing a Destination 9

IV. MIGRATION DATA 9

    SEA Migration Data 10

V. MIGRATION FIELDS 11

    A Generalized In-Migration Field... 13

    A Generalized Out-Migration Field 15

    Net Migration Fields 15

VI. MIGRATION PATTERNS BEFORE 1965 17

VII. RECENT MIGRATION PATTERNS... 18

    Location Preferences 18

    Metropolitan and Nonmetropolitan Population Changes 18

    Spatial Patterns of Net Migration 19

    Characteristics of Growing and Declining Places 21

VIII. DECISIONS UNDERLYING RECENT MIGRATION PATTERNS.. 22

    Exurban Migration Streams... 22

    Migration to More Isolated Nonmetropolitan Places 23

    Migration Down the Urban Hierarchy.. 26

IX. REGIONAL CASE STUDIES 27

    Case Studies Using Aggregate Migration Data.. 27

    Migration to Harrison, Arkansas: A Case Study Using

    Individual Survey Data 29

X. PROSPECT.. 30

    Impacts of New Migration Patterns 30

    What Will Future Migration Patterns Be? 31

BIBLIOGRAPHY 32

    References Cited 32

    Further Reading.. 33

LIST OF FIGURES

1. Natural and Migrational Population Change Components, by State, 1960-1970. 2
2. Relationship Between Various Residential Migrations and County Boundaries 4
3. Relationship Between Mobility and Age, Migrants Between and Within County Boundaries, 1965-1970 5
4. Rankings of States as Potential Places to Live, University of Illinois Students, 1976 7
5. Example of SEA Boundaries 10
6. In- and Out-Migration Fields of the Cleveland, Ohio SEA, 1955-1960 and 1965-1970 12
7. Example of Channelized Flows 14
8. Net Migration Field of the Cleveland, Ohio SEA, 1955-1960 16
9. Net Migration for Nonmetropolitan Counties in Twenty-six Regions, 1950-1960, 1960-1970, and 1970-1973 19
10. Regions of Relative Growth Due to Migration, 1970-1974 20
11. The Atlanta, Georgia Metropolitan SEA and Surrounding Nonmetropolitan SEA's 23
12. Village Population Growth, Kansas, 1950-1970 23
13. Net Migration Fields of Los Angeles, California, 1955-1960 and 1965-1970 25
14. Net Migration Fields of Three Nonmetropolitan SEA's in Arkansas and Mississippi, 1955-1960 and 1965-1970 26
15. Annual Net Migration by County, Vermont, New Hampshire, and Maine, 1960-1970 and 1970-1974 .. 28
16. Annual Net Migration by County, Arkansas, 1960-1970 and 1970-1974 29

LIST OF TABLES

1. Percent Population Change, SMSA's and Nonmetropolitan Areas, 1960-1970 and 1970-1975 18
2. Migration To and From SMSA's, 1965-1970 and 1970-1975 19
3. Migration Between the Atlanta SEA and Neighboring Nonmetropolitan SEA's, 1955-1960 and 1965-1970 23
4. Migration Between Nonmetropolitan SEA's of the Interior West and Selected Metropolitan SEA's, 1955-1960 and 1965-1970 24
5. Migration Between the Chicago SEA and Other Metropolitan SEA's in Illinois, 1955-1960 and 1965-1970 27

I. THE STUDY OF MIGRATION

Migration can be thought of as the movement of people from one residential location to another. Social scientists in many different disciplines have studied migration—perhaps because the idea of choosing a place to live is such a common experience, or perhaps because such decisions have implications for all aspects of life in which social scientists have a valid interest. Economists have approached the study of migration by hypothesizing that people move from one place to another on the basis of job and other economic opportunities. Sociologists and demographers have often studied the population components (sex, age, occupation structures) of groups of migrants and the impacts migration has had upon the population composition of origin and destination areas. Anthropologists commonly study the problems resulting from two groups with different cultural traits and traditions suddenly living in proximity because of migration by one or both groups. Geographers have studied both the spatial patterns of migration streams and the locational decision-making process of potential migrants. Other social scientists have studied the migration behavior of specific groups of people (e.g., gerontologists studying elderly migration).

This paper will draw upon the work of, and consider the viewpoints of many different social scientists. But it will take a distinctively geographic view, focusing upon locational decisions, spatial patterns of migration, changing spatial patterns of population distribution, and the resultant impact upon places. This is because migration is a fundamentally spatial process.

In this approach, two kinds of ideas will be discussed: ideas which apply to individuals and their decision-making behavior, and ideas which generalize about aggregations of people. The traditional approaches to migration study tend to use aggregate ideas and concepts, whereas the individual decision-making approach is relatively recent. Nonetheless, both ideas are necessary for a full explanation of migration, and the two kinds will be interwoven in this paper as we attempt to show how individual location decisions sum to aggregate patterns of population distribution.

The first set of ideas, introduced in the next section, are of the aggregate kind and address the importance of migration relative to other forms of population change in the overall growth or decline of places.

II. MIGRATION AS A COMPONENT OF POPULATION CHANGE

Demographic Equation

Migration is only one way in which the population of places can change. The *demographic equation* is a simple mathematical expression which shows the contribution of different population processes to the population change of a particular area during a specified period of time:

$$P_2 = P_1 + B_{1-2} - D_{1-2} + IM_{1-2} - OM_{1-2}$$

Where: P_2 is the population at time 2
P_1 is the population at a previous time 1
B_{1-2} is the number of people born during the time period between times 1 and 2
D_{1-2} is the number of deaths during that period
IM_{1-2} is the number of in-migrants during that time period

OM_{1-2} is the number of out-migrants during that time period

The equation says that the population of a place at a specified date P_2 (say 1980) is equal to the population at a previous date (P_1) (say 1970) plus or minus changes due to births (fertility), deaths (mortality), and migration during the interim period (1970-1980). In essence, it specifies a population system, usually with geographic boundaries (a county, state, or metropolitan area, for example); then adds to the population persons who enter the system through births or in-migration, and subtracts those who leave the system through death or out-migration. The difference between births and deaths is often referred to as *natural change* and the difference between the in-migration and out-migration is referred to as *net migration*.

Natural and Migrational Population Change

The relative importance of the natural versus the migration components of population change of a place varies with the geographic scale of places examined. At the very broadest scale, taking the world as a whole, there are (as yet) no in- or out-migrants—all population change is accounted for by the relative importance of births and deaths. When we examine population change country by country, natural change remains the dominant component, although there have been very significant population changes in the past because of migration (e.g., European immigration to the U.S. in the late nineteenth century). Very few countries today show either significant percentage growth or percentage decline as a result of migration. There are some fairly large population movements across international boundaries, including "temporary" labor migrations among several European countries, refugees displaced from some African and Asian countries (including hundreds of thousands of Vietnamese to the U.S.), and considerable numbers of illegal immigrants to the U.S. from Mexico and the Caribbean. But most of these movements have not had major importance in either reducing a population problem in the origin country or greatly accentuating a population problem in the destination country (although problems often arise in particular places within the destination country). In sum, the explanation and understanding of contemporary population change from country to country lies in the birth and death rates—the "population numbers problem" in most countries is a problem related to excess births over deaths, not to immigration or emigration.

When we examine population change *within* most countries, however, migration is usually a more important factor than place to place variations in natural change. Within the U.S., place to place variation in net migration is much greater than the variation in either birth or death rates. Figure 1 illustrates this for individual states where natural change 1960-1970 is plotted on the horizontal axis and net migration on the vertical axis. Natural change varies from about eight percent to about twenty-seven percent, whereas net migration varies from minus fifteen percent to nearly plus fifty percent. If no one were to move between states, we would still have differential population growth—those states with younger populations and/or large native (American Indian, Eskimo) populations would grow at the fastest rates. But the variation in growth because of migration is even greater.

Those states which "broke even" because of migration (e.g., Indiana, Oklahoma, Minnesota) can attribute their total growth to natural increases; but there are nonetheless large in-flows and out-flows of migrants and important changes in the composition of the population because of migration. Indiana, for example, has a net in-migration of over 32,000 blacks, considerably increasing the black population of that state, compared to an overall net out-migration of 58,000 (U.S. Bureau of the Census, 1971: 35). Also, as a result of migration, there are places within most states that are growing or declining rapidly, rendering the overall state net migration

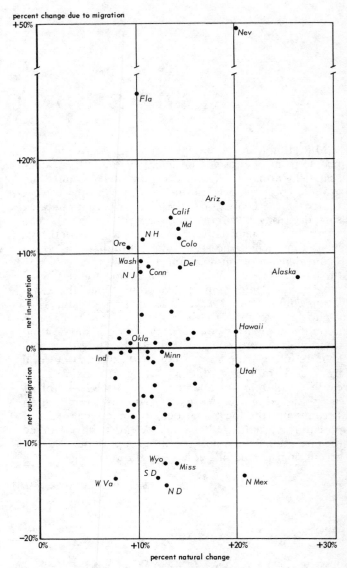

Figure 1. Natural and migrational population change components, by state, 1960-1970. Source: U.S. Bureau of the Census (1971: Table 18).

figure too general for real accuracy, and perhaps somewhat misleading.

At the narrower geographic scale—counties, for instance—there is somewhat greater variation from place to place in natural change than at the state scale; but migration accounts for even greater variations. During the 1960's numerous suburban counties grew at very rapid rates—partly because of large numbers of young families giving birth to many children, but even more because large numbers of people moved into such areas. Conversely, out-migration from many central cities and from isolated rural areas accounted for considerable losses, although the result was a net population increase because of natural change.

At this scale we can illustrate an important principle underlying the demographic equation that helps to clarify the relationships between natural and migrational components of population change. Fertility, mortality, and migration at a place are not independent of each other. The movement of different types of people in and out of an area can alter the natural components of change there, just as the natural change can influence the propensity of a population to migrate. To illustrate, most counties in the U.S. gained through an excess of births over deaths during the 1950's, except for a band of counties extending from southern Iowa, through northern Missouri, into northern Kansas. For decades these agricultural areas had been losing young persons through out-migration (both to regional centers such as Kansas City, Omaha, and Des Moines, and to California), leaving a residual population with an elderly age structure. An excess of deaths over births resulted. Conversely, population increases from natural change have been augmented in places to which young family in-migrants are attracted. Other interrelationships between natural and migrational change will be noted later in this paper.

Our exploration of population redistribution resulting from migration will be conducted largely at a geographic scale narrower than the state level, often using the county as a unit of analysis because it is the smallest geographic unit for which data are readily available. It is critical to understand the migration process at this scale in order to explain population change.

Predicting Components of Population Change

Demographers study all three of the basic population processes (birth, death, and migration) to understand the mechanisms by which the populations of places change through time, usually by looking at past changes, and to make predictions of future populations for planning purposes. We can learn from their efforts.

When examining population change in the past, we can specify the total population at the earlier and later dates ($P_1 + P_2$ in the demographic equation) fairly reliably from census figures, and counts of births and deaths are typically available from vital statistics for the interim period (although all of these are subject to error). The measurement of migration, however, is often difficult. Residential movements across administrative boundaries in the United States are not recorded, as are birth and death statistics within administrative units. (In many countries of the world, especially in Europe, persons moving to a new parish or county are required to register their new address—a procedure which may have undesirable attributes, but which produces excellent migration data!)

Consequently demographers must resort to various ways of estimating migration. One simple method is to calculate the natural change and add (or subtract) that to the earlier population figure (P_1). The result, which is the predicted population at the later date had there been no migration, is then compared to the actual population at P_2; the difference is a net migration figure. A problem encountered in this procedure is that individuals may be born and counted in the total births, then migrate out of the area; just as people may migrate in, then die and be counted in the death figure. Although their numbers can be estimated, actual migrants are not being counted, just a residual "net" total of people who cannot be accounted for as entering or leaving the system through birth or death.

When attempting to estimate the components of population change in the future, a new set of difficulties arises. Births must be predicted on the basis of the past birth rate, estimates of the number of females in the population of childbearing age, and socioeconomic and family characteristics of the population which relate to the propensity of that population to have children. Predictions of deaths are based on the previous death rate, the age structure of the population coupled with knowledge of the death rates of various categories or "cohorts" (we expect a higher overall death rate in a population with greater numbers of people in age cohorts over sixty, for example), and additional information such as socioeconomic and occupational structures. Fairly sophisticated and successful models have been derived for the prediction of births and deaths in the short run.

Prediction of migration in the future for particular places is more difficult. Early approaches to the problem attempted to predict net migration on the basis of labor market conditions (wage levels, composition of the labor force, etc.). Such a model seemed satisfactory in many situations, especially when applied to rural areas. However, the accurate prediction of net migration suffers from the fact that a net migration figure can result from vastly different numbers of migrants. A net figure of 10,000 can be the result of 100,000 in-migrants to a place and 90,000 out-migrants from a place; or equally the result of 10,000 in-migrants and no out-migrants!

The Lowry Hypothesis

Lowry (1966) noted another problem with the attempts to predict net migration. After examining migration among major metropolitan areas in the U.S., he concluded that a better approach would be to predict separately the in- and out-migration components of the net migration total. Using the example of the San Jose, California and Albany, New York metropolitan areas in the 1950's, he showed that in- and out-migration may be responsive to different factors. San Jose, with about the same metropolitan population as Albany in 1960, had a much more favorable economic and job climate in the 1950's and had four times as many in-migrants between 1955 and 1960 (203,000 versus 52,000). Apparently in-migration was related to economic conditions. However, both places had about the same number of out-migrants (Albany with 71,000 and San Jose with 74,000)—apparently out-migrants were not responding to economic conditions. The result, which has become known as the "Lowry Hypothesis," states that: 1) in-migration to a metropolitan area tends to be a function of labor market conditions at that place, with individual migrants responding to job and wage incentives, and 2) out-migration from a metropolitan place is unrelated to labor market conditions there.

More recent studies (Morrison, 1971; Alonso, 1972) have taken up the cause of the Lowry Hypothesis and have shown how out-migration is indeed related to such variables as the age structure of the population (young adult age cohorts being prone to migrate regardless of economic conditions), the percentage of the labor force in manufacturing (manufacturing populations being more stable), and the proportion of the population who are perpetual movers (reflecting the tendency for some people to be "movers," an idea to be discussed later). Other researchers have documented factors which might be related to out-migration and not to in-migration, including the "pull" of nearby places, the size of place, and the proportion of government workers in a place.

Although there is still debate surrounding the Lowry Hypothesis (Trott, 1971; Renshaw, 1974), with some researchers concluding that out-migration does respond significantly to economic conditions (especially in the longer run), it is often preferable to consider the two components of net migration separately. This is because aggregate out-migration from any place is the result of a set of individual decisions *to move* (regardless of destination); whereas total in-migration to a place is the result of a whole set of individual decisions of *where* to move (regardless of origin). These two decisions are often made on the basis of quite different factors, as we will show in the next section.

In this paper we will consider out-migration and in-migration separately whenever possible, but will use net migration when only such data are available, or when a measure of net migration is adequate to make a point about the growth or decline of a place. The next section, then, examines the migration decision and other individual-level ideas which have a bearing upon the understanding of aggregate patterns of migration.

III. MIGRATION DECISION-MAKING

The migration process involves households or individuals making decisions about moving their residences to other locations. A single individual moving from one apartment to another or from one city to another; two single individuals breaking away from their respective households to live together; a family of two adults and one child moving from an apartment to a house; a large family including children, parents, and grandparents moving from one location to another—all can be thought of as part of the migration process. There are a variety of circumstances surrounding individual moves, and there are different degrees of participation of individual migrants in the decision-making process. Some individuals are directly involved in the decision-making process, whereas others, such as small children, do not participate directly in the decision but have their interests taken into account.

The decision to migrate from one place to another is not only a decision to change a specific residential environment (house, yard, neighborhood) but is a decision to relocate the "home base" for the household's *activity space*, that set of places with which the household interacts on a regular basis for work, shopping, recreational, social, or educational purposes. The decision, therefore, represents a change in both the specific site of the household and its relative location.

Traditionally students of migration made a distinction between *local movers*, persons who move within the boundaries of a county, and *migrants*, persons who cross a county boundary while changing residential location. Researchers and planners still use this distinction as a convenient method of counting migrants as they affect the growth or decline of counties. Essentially this is a demographic equation mentality—those migrating into or out of the geographic system (county) are migrants and those staying within (even though they may have changed residence) are not. When considering the decision-making aspects of migration the distinction may have little meaning. In terms of distance moved, for example, a great variation is possible for movers, an even greater variation is possible for migrants, and considerable overlap between the two is possible. In Figure 2 the household migrating from A to B moves a considerably greater distance than the one moving from C to D, yet only the latter is said to have "migrated." The latter is also put in the same category, in the statistics, as the household moving say 500 miles from E to F. Furthermore, there is no guarantee that crossing a county boundary will significantly change the residential environment or the activity space of a household. The definition of "migration" therefore presents difficulties to the researcher interested in specific aspects of the decision-making process.

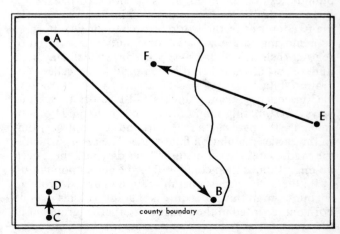

Figure 2. Relationship between various residential migrations and county boundaries.

An alternative way of describing migration makes the distinction between: 1) partial displacement migration— residential moves that disturb only part of the household's activity space and thus are usually local in nature whether or not a boundary is crossed, and 2) total displacement migration—longer distance moves in which not only the residence but also the entire activity space is moved (Roseman, 1971b). This is a satisfying classification because it effectively distinguishes types of moves on the basis of reasons for moving, information sources used in the decision, and impact upon the household. Aggregate data collecting efforts, such as the U.S. census, do not include information on specific moves, much less on activity spaces. Nonetheless such a classification is useful in theory and in studies using individual survey data.

It is important to remember that migration is an act that involves both changing the residential environment and the activity space. We will find later, for instance, that some areas have experienced recent growth because of persons making total displacement migrations, whereas other areas are gaining only because it is possible for persons to move there while moving only part of their activity space in the process (partial displacement migrations). In the latter case persons often choose a nonmetropolitan site, but keep part of their activity space in a metropolitan area. The key to growth for such nonmetropolitan places is their access (within 100 km or so) to urban amenities such as jobs and shopping.

The Decision: To Move

In discussing specifics of the migration decision we shall separate ideas relative to the decision *to move* from ideas related to the decision *where to move*.[1] Although we recognize that the two decisions are often hard to distinguish and are sometimes made simultaneously, thinking about the two separately allows us to learn much about the total migration act.

The decision to leave a place (to move) is often a very ordinary, and even an expected, part of life. In Western society there are regularities in individual and family *life cycles*. At key points in that life cycle, decisions to move are very common. An individual often leaves home upon graduation from high school to form a new single-person household. With marriage one or two moves usually occur. As a family expands, housing needs often change, again causing a decision to move. (American middle- and upper-middle-class young couples typically move from an apartment to a house when they have children—even to a larger home when the family expands further.) When children grow up, older couples may move into smaller quarters as a result of this key change in housing needs. Separations and divorces, or other changes in family structure, similarly lead to one or more moves.

Career cycle factors are likewise related to migration. The procurement of an initial job upon college or high school graduation, job transfers, lay-offs, or even pro-

[1] Brown and Moore (1970) use this distinction in their model of intraurban migration decisions.

motions to a better job in a different location can be related directly to residential movement. Job promotions may indirectly cause migration by supplying the needed financial boost for a family to move to a new dwelling. Similarly, an upwardly mobile family often attempts to "match" the status of its dwelling and neighborhood to the status of a new job. Finally, retirement frees people of one key element in the activity space— the work place—and provides additional leisure time, thus typically stimulating thoughts of migration.

An age/mobility graph (Figure 3) illustrates the result of these life and career cycle factors. For migrants who stay within a given county, as well as for those who cross county boundaries, the greatest mobility occurs in the age cohorts between twenty and thirty-four years. People are going through many of the key points in both cycles during this time. Those factors relating to longer distance (total displacement) migrations, such as going off to college or taking a job after high school, come somewhat earlier than those relating to local moves, such as family formation and expansion or job promotion—hence the difference in the curves for the two types of migrations.

The graph also shows that along with this large group of migrants goes a set of secondary migrants, their children in the age cohort five to nine years. One can also see an increase in the mobility rate for between-county migrants in the sixty-five to sixty-nine age cohort which includes many persons at the retirement point in the life cycle, and in the very elderly age cohorts where many persons are leaving their own homes for institutions or homes of children or other relatives.

Other decisions to move have little to do with life or career cycles. Some are essentially *forced migrations* that result from inner city urban renewal projects, highway construction, or dam-reservoir projects. In such cases the decision to move is not made by those who migrate, but by a governmental body. The decision on where to

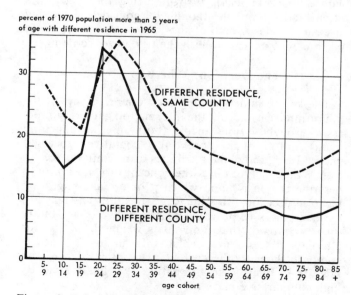

Figure 3. Relationship between mobility and age, migrants between and within county boundaries, 1965-1970. Source: U.S. Bureau of the Census (1973: Table 193).

move is left to the individual—such persons, in effect, become refugees.

Still other decisions to move are related to perceived neighborhood conditions. Threats to property values, to the safety of their neighborhoods, or to school quality have put some families in a position of feeling little choice but to move. On the other hand, many of the poor or minority persons may feel so threatened, but in effect feel that there is no choice but to stay because they lack the knowledge about places to go.

There is one final important element in the decision to move. It has been said (and often by the Census Bureau) that about twenty percent of the American population moves every year, tempting the conclusion that everyone moves every five years. But such estimates are counting moves, not movers, and single individuals may account for more than one of the moves. During any given period of a few years, we have a set of "movers" and a larger set of "stayers." This is the *mover/stayer* concept, stating that a minority of individuals—movers—accounts for most of the moves in a population (Morrison, 1971). This concept holds in many countries having different societies and different levels of development.

Accounting for this concept, in part, are the large numbers of people in the very mobile age range of eighteen to thirty-six years and the moves associated with key life cycle points. Also accounting for this are some persons who just seem to move a lot! They come from all socioeconomic categories and racial groups, but may be persons who are somehow unsettled (or unsettleable), perhaps occupationally unstable or socially restless. It has been observed that a person or family is most likely to move again right after having moved (except for persons making the major investment of purchasing a home) and the probability of moving again declines with time at a given place. As people establish social and economic roots in a neighborhood or community, they tend to stay in that place. As familiarity with a place increases through living there, loyalties often increase and the thought of considering moving elsewhere fades. Some of the movers, then, are those persons who never establish the ties, never settle in.

The Decision: Where to Move

The key to understanding the "where" aspect of the migration decision is in the information gathering process. Through various media (both interpersonal and mass) and through more direct cognitive processes, people learn about the attributes of potential places to live. Wolpert (1965) uses the concept of *place utility* to describe the basis upon which people make migration location decisions. It is the value (or utility) assigned to various places as potential places to live. Place utility theory contends that individuals weigh this value for alternate places about which information is known, compare them to the current place of residence, and migrate to one of the alternatives if it has sufficiently high comparative place utility.

People use numerous criteria to judge places, but these are always conditioned by the potential migrants' general knowledge of places and their ability to gather further information as part of the search process. Two types of information ultimately weigh upon the location decision: 1) information that people gather throughout their lifetime to form a general set of long-term place preferences—they gather such information and assign place utilities or location preferences without necessary reference to migration; and 2) information that people gather about places, often a limited number of places, when they seriously contemplate a move. These latter places are called the *search space*.

The two types of informational inputs to the migration decision—long-term place preferences and search spaces—are discussed in turn, followed by a discussion of the factors relating to the choice of one particular place as a destination.

Long-Term Place Preferences

People are continually acquiring and storing information about places. Some is locational information—where places are with reference to other places or with respect to some other reference system (direction, distance, country, region, etc.).[2] Also stored is information about the content of places—major landscape elements, population characteristics, and other attributes that might have a bearing upon "what it is like to live there." These combine with locational attributes to form a total site and situation image of potential places to live.

Geographers and others have attempted to measure these images over the last few years. A common research procedure is to ask people to evaluate different neighborhoods in a city or different states in the United States as potential places to live. The result is then mapped as a *preference map* (often referred to as a *mental map*). In this procedure people place their evaluations next to the name of each neighborhood or state on the research assumption (perhaps not unrealistic) that individuals attach meaning to language symbols or place names.[3]

Figure 4 is an example of a preference map exercise given to a sample of University of Illinois undergraduate students in early 1976. They were given a list of state names and asked to rank the six most desirable as a place to live and the six least desirable. Most of the students grew up in Illinois, sixty-two percent in the Chicago suburbs. Their preference for the West Coast, Colorado, and Illinois is apparent, as is their dislike for the prospect of living in the Great Plains or the Deep South.[4]

---

[2] It is argued that formal education in the United States is presently lacking because location, or "place name" geography is not taught in elementary and secondary schools as it used to be. Today's young adult population is said to be locationally ignorant, not knowing where Vietnam or India is located, not to mention Attica or Anchorage.

[3] The alternative is to give people outline maps of the area in question and have them evaluate places as they perceive them on the map. This is as much a test of their locational knowledge as it is of their preference for places. A combination of the two methods is, of course, possible.

[4] This pattern is typical of that found in similar studies. Gould and White (1974), for example, found positive images of the West Coast, Colorado, plus the home states for students in Minnesota and Pennsylvania, and California. These groups were also unanimous in their aversion to living in the Plains States and the South. Alabama students

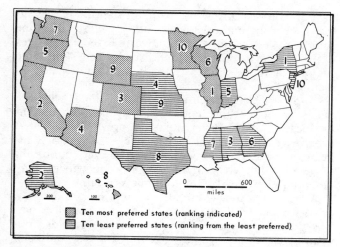

Figure 4. Rankings of states as potential places to live, University of Illinois students, 1976. Source: compiled by author.

In attaching attributes to place names, individuals have a tendency to make *spatial stereotypes*—viewing the entire place (e.g., the state) as having the characteristics of one particular spot they know about, or in any case generalizing specific information beyond the area which is known (e.g., generalizing about the Midwest on the basis of one visit to Ashtabula, Ohio). To illustrate, the same survey that resulted in Figure 4 was given to similar samples of University of Illinois students in 1970, 1971, and 1972. The results were nearly identical with those of 1976 except that New York was consistently in the top ten desired places in the earlier surveys but was rated last in 1976. The 1976 class had just been exposed to several months of extensive media coverage of the fiscal problems in New York City. To these students, the language symbol "New York" came to be identified with serious problems and the entire state as a place to live suffered in their preference maps.

Partly because of the tendency to stereotype, the geographic scale at which preference maps are measured has a significant bearing upon the outcome. If we had asked the sample individuals to respond to symbols such as "New Orleans," "southern California," "San Francisco," "northern Michigan," or "Baltimore," the overall preference maps could have come out differently. To many people, those parts of states conjure quite different images from their respective state images as a whole.

There are several information gathering processes that can play an important role in forming preference maps. As suggested above, exposure to mass media is one of them. The geographic content of television news and entertainment, newspapers, magazines, movies, books, and recordings all, in the long run, help to shape preference maps. One of the reasons New York City's fiscal woes received so much exposure relates to its position at the top of the urban hierarchy and its associated central position in the dissemination of news and information (headquarters for television and radio networks, wire services, and publishing activities). Tradi-

tionally there has been a large volume of information emanating from New York City—when the news is bad a bad image is spread far and wide. Other forms of mass communication enhance place images by repeated mention or coverage of particular places. Popular recordings in the U.S., for example, have gone through locational fads that at various times emphasize such places as New Orleans, "Philly," "Motown" (Detroit), California, Georgia, West Virginia, and the Rocky Mountains.[5]

Information for preference maps can be obtained through other mechanisms, including travel experiences, discussions with others about their travel and residential experiences, and formal educational experiences. Travel may be particularly important since seeing places firsthand tends to make them more "real" to many people. As leisure time for Americans has increased, more vacation travel has ensued, and the relationship between vacation travel experiences and choosing a place to live has probably increased (a topic we will explore later).

We do not yet know the extent to which these general preference maps are directly important to migration decisions.[6] We do know that, at a very general level, places that get high preference ratings, such as California, Colorado, and Florida, have been growing rapidly because of migration. We also know that preference images influence the growth or decline of certain categories of places. For example, there is a propensity for whites migrating from greater than, say, 100 km, to avoid central cities in metropolitan areas which have high percentages of black population, high crime rates, and other social and environmental problems. However, whites moving from the suburbs are not so affected (Roseman, 1976). This is probably because whites migrating longer distances tend to stereotype the *entire* central city as undesirable as a result of undesirable attributes of parts of that central city. Nearby potential migrants, on the other hand, can distinguish between different parts of the central city and do not avoid it entirely.

Since there are many other factors that influence the decision of where to move, general preference maps do not necessarily predict where an individual will locate. The first tangible act in the decision is to begin a search after having made at least a tentative decision to move. By understanding this search process we can shed light upon some of the other factors.

Search Spaces

The set of places that the potential migrant seriously considers is a *search space* (Brown and Moore, 1970). The concept is best discussed at two different geographic scales: a broad national or regional scale for persons considering a move from one locale (city, town, or rural area) to another; and the local scale for potential migrants within a city, town, or local area.

At the broader scale, search spaces may be geographically extensive or severely constrained. Single persons upon graduating from college may have several job pos-

show a more egocentric locational preference by choosing the Deep South and California above all other places.

[5] See Francaviglia (1973) and Ford (1971) for discussions of locational aspects of popular music production.
[6] For a discussion of this issue see Lloyd (1976).

sibilities and even several job offers at a variety of locations. Their perceived lack of ties to a place, coupled with a drive to see other places, may allow serious consideration of all these locations. Their actual choice could be highly influenced by that idealized preference map which they have been fashioning over the years.

More realistically, however, might be the case where only a few feasible places are included in the search spaces. As a matter of fact, in a survey of 696 migrants during the early 1960's, Lansing and Mueller (1967: 211) found that sixty-four percent did not consider any alternative to the place they actually chose! The migration decision was essentially a choice between the former residential location and one other. Many of these persons with such limited search spaces were transferred by their employers, others had lined up a job before moving, and still others had gathered information regarding jobs only at that particular place. The decision of where to move is made simultaneously with the decision to move in many of these instances.

Millions of migrants, both black and white, used limited search spaces during the last several decades in moving from the rural South to the East, Midwest, and West Coast. They usually based their choice of destination not on having a specific job prospect, but upon the lure of friends and relatives who had migrated previously to a particular city. These friends were the only information source (defining a one-location search space) and often helped to cushion the shock of entering the urban environment by helping the migrants to find a job, sometimes even by housing the new arrival for a time. Many such migrants gave no thought to moving to any other place. This dependency upon friends and relatives has been typical of immigrants to the United States as well.

Often migrants go back to the place where they grew up or where their family roots are found. These *return migrants* have limited their search spaces to and made their locational decision on the basis of a place about which they have knowledge through previous residential experience. Again, limited search spaces are the rule.

Retirees also tend to have limited search spaces. At the retirement stage of the life and career cycles, many persons are moving to locations in a better environment (e.g., nice climate), but do not define large search spaces across broad areas with desirable environments (e.g., the entire "Sun Belt"). Instead they depend upon their own travel experiences, moving to that place where they had been vacationing annually for numerous years, the reasons for choosing a place to live converging with the reasons for choosing a vacation spot. This is illustrated by the findings of a recent study of persons migrating to Florida (Sly, 1974). Of 1333 migrants interviewed, 984 (about seventy-four percent) had visited Florida one or more times prior to moving to that state. Of those 984, about two-thirds traveled to Florida for vacations (as opposed to business trips, visiting family or friends, etc.) and almost ninety percent of the travel experiences in Florida were for more than one week. Other retirees depend upon friends and relatives to define their search spaces. Numerous retirement communities in Arizona, Florida, and elsewhere lure retired persons from the

East or Midwest through a chain information process in which friends influence each other. One person or couple makes the move, then advertises the advantages of the new environment to their friends. Thus, long-time friends (or relatives) can retire at the same locale and maintain close social contact.

It appears that search spaces at a national scale are indeed limited for the majority of migrants. The residential location of friends and relatives, previous residential experience, and travel experiences, all factors influencing general preference, seem to be very important in defining limited search spaces beyond which many potential migrants do not continue searching.

When migration within a local area is considered, a greater number of alternative locations typically comprises the search space. Using newspaper want ads, consulting real estate agents, soliciting friends' and relatives' opinions and assistance, and literally searching by visiting potential sites, are all processes that influence the search space. Information sources that depend upon others (friends, relatives, real estate agents) play a very important role. The cognitive preference maps of others, formed on the basis of their experiences in the local area, can greatly influence a search space.[7]

This is particularly true of migrants who are arriving from a different locale and must, in addition to choosing a locale, choose a specific site within. Such persons have two search spaces—one at the broader geographic scale (national or regional) and one at the scale of the local area of the destination. The second search space typically must depend upon the preference maps of others, often resulting in the choice of a residence which turns out to be undesirable because of the limited input of the migrants' own preferences. The result is that such migrants frequently move again within a year or two within that local area.

Locational constraints are instrumental in defining the local search space. The principal work place of the household may be used as a reference point around which a maximum radius is defined for including locations in the search space. In small communities and cities up to 200,000 or so population, this radius may encompass the entire community, but in larger metropolitan areas this is likely to limit the search space to one part of the metropolitan area.[8] Perhaps a more realistic idea of the workplace as a locational constraint is that a radius is defined within which potential migrants are indifferent to distance to the workplace, and beyond which distance to work is traded off with other attributes of the potential residential site. In this case, successively greater distances to work beyond the critical radius will be acceptable only for sites with greater and greater attractiveness (in terms of cost, neighborhood environment, character of the home, etc.).[9]

[7] See Palm, (1976) for an examination of the influence of real estate agents upon search spaces.

[8] Adams (1969) has argued that general mental maps, search spaces, and migrant destinations within metropolitan areas tend to be limited to sectors radiating outward from the center partly as a result of the structure of transportation systems in cities and the associated resistance to travel across the center of the city.

[9] This idea is akin to the *frictionless zone* concept suggested by Getis (1969).

In individual cases, location with respect to places of other regular activity might limit the household search space. Access to certain types of schools, shopping facilities, and church or club locations, for example, may be important enough to a household so that they "screen" locations initially on the basis of these factors.

Other constraints are economical and racial. The realities of American urban life are that the poor are quite limited in their search spaces—limited to private or public low-cost housing. Similarly, most minority individuals are excluded from vast areas both within major central cities and especially in suburban areas. This puts a particular hardship on low income and minority blue-collar workers whose jobs have moved from central city areas to suburban areas with the recent out-migration of industry. It is difficult for them to commute outward, given the structure of public transportation systems in American cities, and difficult for them to move their residences outward.[10]

Choosing a Destination

The choice of one place for residence out of those comprising the search space is the last decision in the migration act. At the broad geographic scale, acquiring a job or a job transfer may almost dictate that choice, as it dictated the search space. For other migrants, job-related reasons and the attraction of urban amenities have always been important, but on the increase are reasons related to climate, recreational opportunities, and rural life-style.[11] Later in this paper we will explore how these reasons for choosing a destination have had important impacts uopn the differential growth of places over the last several decades.

At the narrower (local) scale, choosing that one destination is usually an act of matching the household needs and desires to a place, subject to job location, and racial or economic constraints. Household needs and desires are clearly related to life and career cycles—hence, the decisions to move and where to move have close affinity. This is one of the processes by which relatively homogeneous neighborhoods, defined on the basis of income, ethnicity, and stage in the life cycle, for example, tend to develop and to characterize our metropolitan areas.

Brown and Holmes (1971) have also suggested that in the final decision, at the local level, the place chosen tends to be near the center of the search space. If this is so, the search process may be one of searching around the ideal location to confirm that the final choice is actually the best (at least the best in a locational sense, or near the center of that broader environment that is preferred).

[10] See Muller (1976) and Stutz (1977) for detailed commentaries on these problems.

[11] For a discussion of recreation/amenity factors in migration see Svart (1976).

IV. MIGRATION DATA

Numerous sources of data are available to social scientists in the United States for the study of migration behavior and the resultant spatial patterns of migration. The ideal way to study individual migration behavior, including reasons for the decision to move, formation of search space, and reasons for choosing a particular destination, is to survey a large number of persons via questionnaire or personal interview. Surveys on a large scale, however, are rare largely because of the great cost involved. As a result, most survey research has been somewhat limited in sample size and is usually location-specific in the sense that only migration *within* or *to* a specific locality is studied.

Assuming that the researcher is interested only in movers (and not stayers),[12] it is inefficient to use random samples of an entire population to isolate only migrants. Instead, researchers typically use various other methods to initiate the identification of movers who are subsequently surveyed. For example, lists of new customers are often obtainable from utility companies (gas, elec-tric, and water companies). These lists typically contain only households who have moved *into* the community served by the company, giving the researcher a list of persons with a common migration destination from a variety of origins (a type of *in-migration field* to be discussed shortly). Sometimes similar lists are obtainable from local "welcome wagon" representatives who combine utility lists with other sources to identify new arrivals.

Occasionally, lists of persons changing address within a community can be obtained from utility companies, but more commonly used sources for such data are telephone and city directories. It is possible to take a sample (or deal with the entire listed population if the community is small) of persons listed at time t and look for them at time t + 1 (say, one or two years later). Those who are found at the same address are non-movers, those found at a new address are local movers, those who are not found are either out-migrants, persons who died, persons who changed their names through marriage or other processes, or persons who are just no longer listed (those who drop telephone service for example). The reverse process can be followed by

[12] Perhaps a weakness in contemporary migration research is a preoccupation with movers, with less attention being paid to factors that influence the stability of significant proportions of the population.

tracing persons backward in time and identifying the alternative outcomes, including this time, the identification of possible in-migrants to the community.

Another source is the use of post office forwarding address cards (or lists made from the cards) which are in the public domain and which identify local moves plus the forwarding address of persons moving *out* of the community. This latter feature makes this source unique and potentially valuable to researchers.

All of the above migration data sources are subject to very important biases. Most are biased against the poor and/or minorities and, in addition, are less accurate and less easily obtainable in large cities. Yet the use of these sources and other methods of obtaining survey data are valuable to migration researchers in their efforts to understand migration behavior.

Broad patterns of migration, however, are virtually impossible to obtain through survey methods. We must rely upon large-scale government sponsored data gathering efforts. One example is the one percent Social Security survey, which is done yearly and provides information on the migration of persons employed or looking for employment and subject to Social Security taxes.[13] The advantage of these data is that we can get yearly pictures of migration flows within the U.S.; but disadvantages include the fact that the workplace and not the residence is specified, only persons on Social Security are sampled (leaving out federal government workers, many state employees, railroad workers, and some other employment groups) and, because the sample is so small, movement can be specified only between relatively large geographic areas (e.g., states or large metropolitan areas).

Another prominent data source is the U.S. Bureau of the Census, which provides net migration estimates yearly by county (to be discussed and used later in this paper) plus a variety of migration information from the decennial censuses. From the 1960 and 1970 censuses, a sample of the population five years of age and older was asked where they lived five years ago (i.e., on April 1, 1970 they were asked where they lived on April 1, 1965).[14] The Bureau then compiles and publishes the information in a variety of ways. For instance, for local areas (including counties, cities, and census tracts within larger cities) the tabulations include the number of persons living in 1) the same house, 2) a different house but in the same county, 3) a different county, 4) a different state, and 5) a different country. From these tabulations we can get a broad picture of the number and sources of migrants arriving at a place, and in turn some help in explaining the migration component of population growth or decline of that place.

The Bureau of the Census also aggregates these data into large *migration matrices,* or flows among a set of geographic areas. A very useful one is the matrix of

flows between 510 state economic areas (SEA's), which are aggregations of counties and include the entire area of the United States (U.S. Bureau of the Census, 1967, 1972). One weakness of these data is that small flows must be interpreted with caution because of sampling error (Thompson, 1974). Another is that the data are only an indirect measure of migration, as an individual may have moved several times in the five-year period among several places, or an individual may have migrated from a place and then returned during the time interval. In both cases actual migrations are undercounted. The data really represent aggregate population displacement from place to place over a five-year period, regardless of the kind or number of individual migration acts that underlie that displacement.

The strength of these data lies in their specification of flows from place to place for relatively small areas, especially SEA's. In essence, they represent the best "geographic matrix" of migration data available for the United States. We will make use of the SEA migration matrix in this paper to help describe patterns of migration and changes in these patterns between 1955-1960 and 1965-1970.

SEA Migration Data

The Census Bureau has used SEA's for enumeration of migration and other data since 1950. The United States is divided into 510 SEA's, 205 of which are "metropolitan" and the remainder "nonmetropolitan." Figure 5 shows the SEA's for Colorado, typical of the

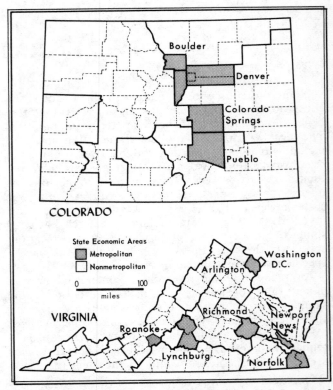

Figure 5. Example of SEA boundaries. Source: U.S. Bureau of the Census (1972).

[13] These data are described in Thompson (1974). Comments on their use can be found in Hirschberg (1971) and U.S. Social Security Administration (1971).

[14] The Bureau used a twenty-five percent sample in 1960 and a fifteen percent sample in 1970. The 1950 census used a similar procedure but asked people where they lived one year previously, making the resultant migration data not directly comparable to the 1960 or 1970 data.

SEA's in the western part of the country, and for Virginia, typical of the East. Metropolitan SEA's were originally defined as those counties which were in metropolitan areas in 1950 (now referred to as Standard Metropolitan Statistical areas or SMSA's). However, where a state boundary divided the metropolitan area, two separate SEA's were created (as in the case of Arlington, Virginia becoming a separate SEA from Washington, D.C. and the suburban Washington parts of Maryland, even though all three areas were considered part of the single Washington metropolitan area). It is also noteworthy that new counties have been added to SMSA's but not to metropolitan SEA's, so that comparison of SEA's through time is possible. Most states have some urban SEA's encompassing one or more counties associated with the major cities of the state.

The Bureau of the Census divided the remainder of each state into nonmetropolitan SEA's using the criteria of economic and agricultural similarity. Usually SEA's are sets of contiguous counties, but in some cases are split into two parts. They have varying shapes and sizes,

and contain a number of counties (ranging from one to dozens of counties but typically having about ten). In the West they tend to cover vast areas where counties are large, and relatively smaller areas in the East where counties are smaller and population density is greater.

In spite of the variation, the coverage of the U.S. is exhaustive and the researcher is presented with the possibility of examining migration flows among and between metropolitan and nonmetropolitan places. One problem does lie in the size of the data matrix; with 510 areal units, there are 259,590 possible flows between different places![15] With modern computer techniques it is possible to "boil down" or summarize all of these flows into generalized patterns; but in this paper, we will demonstrate and utilize a much simpler system of examining flows in the matrix, the *migration field*, which can be done easily without the aid of computer methods.

[15] $510 \times 509 = 259,590$ flows when the diagonal of the migration matrix (i.e., those "flows" which originate and end within an SEA) are not considered. When they are, the total number of flows in the matrix is $510 \times 510 = 260,100$.

V. MIGRATION FIELDS

Since we suspect that factors affecting in-migration and out-migration are somewhat different, we often treat the geographic components of the two separately. This can be done when breaking down a migration data matrix into migration fields.

Figure 6 shows what is referred to as the *in-migration field* of the Cleveland SEA, 1955-1960. It is simply a map of all of those SEA's, both metropolitan and nonmetropolitan, which contribute more than a specified number of migrants to Cleveland. One percent of the total in-migration to Cleveland was chosen as the cutoff level. We now have a picture of the geographic pattern of the major sources of the 145,931 migrants who were in Cleveland in 1960 but not 1955.

A social scientist might be interested in the in-migration component of the population change of Cleveland, and can help to explain it or predict it by knowing something about: 1) the characteristics of the people who move in, and 2) the places, and types of places, from which they came. The latter is captured in the in-migration field concept and is particularly important to the geographer because distance moved, types of environments at the origin and destination, and other aspects of the locational decision are reflected in these aggregate patterns.

Figure 6 also shows the 1965-1970 in-migration field for Cleveland. Comparing it with the 1955-1960 field illustrates an important concept of migration—that over time aggregate flows of migration at this broad scale tend to be rather stable. The in-migration patterns changed little—Boston, for instance, exceeded the cutoff in 1965-1970 (and hence appeared on the map), but was

just below the cutoff in 1955-1960 with 1404 migrants to Cleveland. Los Angeles and a nonmetropolitan SEA in Virginia also appeared in 1965-1970. One of the reasons, in this case, for the stability is that Cleveland's overall attraction for in-migrants changed little between the two time periods (145,931 in-migrants in 1955-1960 and 149,712 in 1965-1970). We shall see later that where a migration component of growth at a place changes dramatically, it is likely that significant changes in the geographic patterns of flows to or from that place have occurred.

Out-migration fields for Cleveland are also shown in Figure 6, and are defined as that set of SEA's which received from the Cleveland SEA more than a specified number of migrants during the time period. They too have stability over time.

Most of the total volume of migration within the United States is either among metropolitan SEA's or between them and nonmetropolitan SEA's, with relatively few migrants moving among nonmetropolitan SEA's. Because of this, most of the general patterns, and changes in the patterns, can be observed by looking at metropolitan migration fields (such as those for Cleveland). When we examine such fields for 1955-1960 and 1965-1970, certain recurring patterns are observable and can be generalized in the following ways.[16]

[16] The author has examined the in- and out-migration fields of all 205 metropolitan SEA's for 1965-1970 and a substantial portion of those for 1955-1960. They were generated by a computer mapping program written by Richard E. Groop of the University of Kansas, whose assistance is gratefully acknowledged. The models discussed in this paper resulted from the synthesis of all the migration field patterns observed.

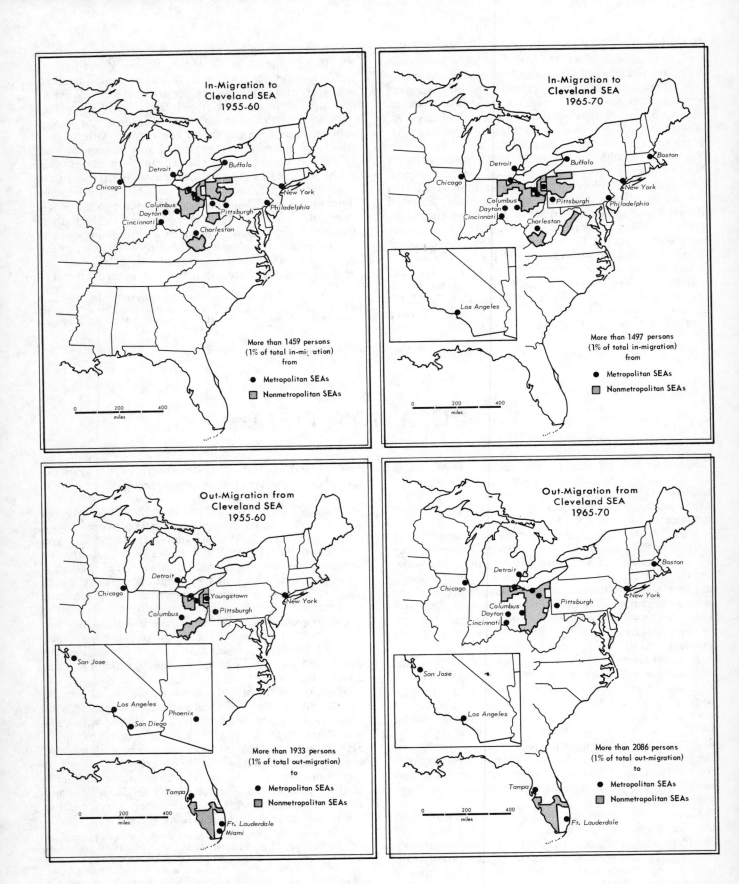

Figure 6. In- and out-migration fields of the Cleveland, Ohio SEA, 1955-1960 and 1965-1970. Source: U.S. Bureau of the Census (1967, 1972).

A Generalized In-Migration Field

A generalized description of in-migration fields includes three identifiable spatial patterns which appear consistently in the fields of U.S. metropolitan areas. The first may be referred to as *hinterland migration,* the tendency for all cities to draw migrants from their surrounding nonurban territory. The nonmetropolitan SEA's in northern Ohio and northwestern Pennsylvania that contribute large numbers of migrants to Cleveland (Figure 6) are examples. Such migration is partly a function of information disseminated about job opportunities and other attractions of metropolitan places through mass media. Television and radio market areas and newspaper circulation areas tend to correspond to the area of significant hinterland migration.

We can also relate hinterland migration to the contact that people have with urban areas through regular shopping, entertainment, and business trips. Hence, when many nonmetropolitan residents contemplate the decision to move, the search space and ultimate decision of where to go is strongly influenced by the dominance of a nearby metropolitan place in much of their everyday life. Hinterland migration from relatively close range (say up to 100 km) is not as great as might be expected because of the tendency for many persons in small towns and rural areas to substitute commuting for migration (Holmes, 1972). Many individuals retain nonurban residences while taking advantage of metropolitan job opportunities through commuting.

The exact spatial form of hinterland migration, of course, varies from city to city, but certain tendencies are observable. As distance increases from the metropolitan place, its influence decreases and hinterland migration decreases in volume. This *distance decay* pattern is often modified by barriers such as major mountain ranges, water bodies, or state boundaries. In the last case, persons living near state boundaries often "look toward" a major city in their own state for media information and other purposes, and hence may be more likely to migrate there even though a similar-sized or larger city in an adjacent state is closer. In general, the role of such barriers to hinterland migration patterns is analogous to their role in modifying spatial patterns of innovation diffusion.[17]

Another variation is in the areal size of hinterland patterns, which is related to the competition among cities for territorial influence. In areas where large cities are closely spaced, such as the Megalopolis region from Boston to Washington, hinterland migration areas are quite small, because of the severe competition among the various cities for the attraction of migrants. In the West, by contrast, hinterland patterns of such cities as Denver, Salt Lake City, and Albuquerque cover much larger spaces which, of course, are much less densely populated. From the viewpoint of the potential migrant in a nonmetropolitan area choosing a destination city, the concept of *intervening opportunities* may explain the choice of the nearest city—a city which may be quite far away if there are few or no intervening alternatives from which to choose.[18]

A second part of the generalized in-migration field can be termed *intraurban migration.* There is an unmistakable importance of other metropolitan areas in the migration fields of all metropolitan SEA's, important flows coming from all nearby metropolitan SEA's and from larger ones at greater distances. This pattern represents movement through the hierarchy of urban areas, with the population of the sending area being directly related to the number of migrants sent and distance being inversely related to the number.[19] Intraurban migration represents the reality that there are large numbers of migrants generated by all metropolitan areas and their choices of destinations are influenced by their general images of other cities which, in turn, are structured by their location in the urban hierarchy. This is partly because position in the urban hierarchy is related to prominence in the mass media.

Considering the Cleveland in-migration field (Figure 6), most of the nearby Ohio and western Pennsylvania metropolitan areas, regardless of size, show up along with larger cities (but not smaller ones) at greater distances (e.g., Philadelphia, New York City, Boston, Chicago, and Los Angeles). To cite another example, the medium-sized California city of Fresno captures in its in-migration field *all* metropolitan areas in California, larger and medium-sized metropolitan areas elsewhere in the West (e.g., Portland, Seattle, Denver, Salt Lake City), but only the largest at greater distances away (Chicago and New York City).

A third general type of in-migration may be referred to as *channelized* migration, or the tendency for cities to draw from one or two nonmetropolitan areas at greater distances than hinterland migration. Channelized migration results from strong family and friendship ties which have drawn migrants from a particular nonmetropolitan place to a metropolitan area in their search for jobs (Roseman, 1971a). In larger destination cities, these migrants often initially migrated to get a job, then wrote back to relatives and friends indicating their success and encouraging others to follow.

The dependence upon interpersonal information and aid results in one-place search spaces for migrants who are involved in channelized flows. For this reason, large channelized flows easily traverse long distances—that is, potential migrants may not even consider alternative destinations so comparative place utilities based on distance (travel cost, travel time) do not enter the decision-making process. Also, because of the dependence upon interpersonal communication, channelized flows tend to be stable over time. Thus a social system develops in which family and friendship ties remain strong between the two widely separated places, stimulating migration continuously.

---

[17] For a discussion of barriers that affect diffusion patterns see Gould (1969).

[18] The intervening opportunities concept was originated by Stouffer (1940). It is revised and discussed by Stouffer (1960) and Lee (1966).

[19] This idea is formally stated by the *gravity* model: $M_{ij} = P_i P_j / D_{ij}^2$; where M_{ij} is the predicted number of migrants between place i and place j, P_i and P_j are the populations of the two places, and D_{ij} is the distance between them. A thorough discussion of the model can be found in Abler, Adams, and Gould (1971: 221-230).

13

An interesting result of channelization is that the idea of moving to a particular distant urban area diffuses outward from the initial place of origin. For instance, the idea of moving to Muncie, a manufacturing city in Indiana, probably started in the small town of Jamestown, Tennessee, then over the years was passed on by word of mouth to neighboring towns and rural areas until today the channelized component of Muncie's in-migration field covers a large part of east-central Tennessee.

Channelized flows are particularly characteristic of migration from the rural South, which exported millions of migrants, both white and black, from the 1910's until the 1960's. Relatively few job opportunities in the South, combined with changing primary industries (agriculture, mining) that gradually employed fewer and fewer persons, led people to make decisions to move. The decision of where to move depended greatly upon interpersonal information resulting in one-place search spaces and, in turn, aggregate channelized flows. Most metropolitan areas from the Midwest (Minnesota, Iowa, and Missouri on the west) to the Northeast (as far as New York and Boston) have channelized connections with the South (Figure 7). Midwest cities tend to draw from Arkansas, Louisiana, Tennessee, Alabama, and

Mississippi, whereas East Coast cities typically draw from the Carolinas and Georgia. Cleveland (Figure 6) has a rather persistent channelized flow from southern West Virginia.

As suggested by Figure 7, metropolitan areas elsewhere, too, have channelized flows. The in-migration fields of Los Angeles and some of the other West Coast cities have channelized components from Arkansas, Texas, and Louisiana, and some also have channelized flows from the Plains states of the Dakotas, Nebraska, Kansas, and Oklahoma dating from the Dust Bowl days in the 1930's when thousands of people left agriculture in that region for the West Coast. An occasional channelized flow is found elsewhere—the flow from southern Montana to Minneapolis/St. Paul is an example. In general, the only urban in-migration fields which tend not to have channelized flows from distant nonmetropolitan places are the in-migration fields of cities in the South.

In-migration fields occasionally contain an "oddball" flow that cannot be explained as hinterland, urban, or channelized, the three basic patterns discussed above. These tend not to persist over time (and using the SEA migration matrix would be typically seen in 1955-1960 and not 1965-1970 or vice versa). They result from large

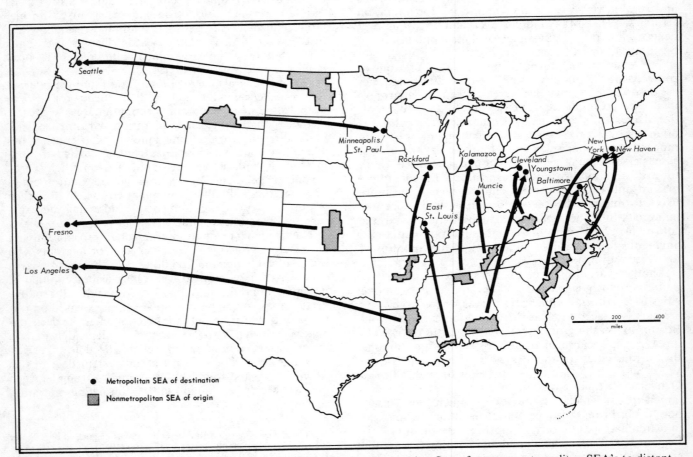

Figure 7. Example of channelized flows. These are relatively large migration flows from nonmetropolitan SEA's to distant metropolitan SEA's which persisted for the periods 1955-1960 and 1965-1970. The persistence suggests that they are based on strong information ties between origin and destination, and therefore are probably channelized flows. These are only a few of the hundreds of channelized flows that probably exist in the U.S. Source: U.S. Bureau of the Census (1967, 1972).

industrial transfers, military transfers, or some other short-term stimulus for migration in which the migrant may have little choice of destination. In general, however, the first three patterns identified go a long way toward describing the in-migration field patterns of U.S. metropolitan areas and also shed some light upon the underlying behavior of migrants.

A Generalized Out-Migration Field

Three major patterns are also characteristic of metropolitan out-migration fields: hinterland, interurban, and recreation/amenity migration. Just as metropolitan areas relate to their surrounding hinterland through mass media, travel behavior and in-migration, they also send large numbers of migrants to nearby nonmetropolitan areas. Cleveland, for example (Figure 6), sends large numbers of persons to nonmetropolitan areas in northern Ohio. Some of the migrants making up such streams are persons returning "home" after having lived in the metropolitan area for periods of time up to several decades. Others seek job opportunities or the life-style of small towns and rural areas and choose a destination within the area of influence of the metropolitan place in which they grew up. Some are *exurban* migrants who are still tied to the metropolitan area by commuting to jobs, retail stores, social functions, and recreational activities. They make partial displacement migrations that do not completely change their activity spaces. Other exurban migrants go beyond distances that would allow direct contact with the metropolitan area but may still have ties through radio, television, or newspapers.[20] Exurban migrants are particularly important to present day migration patterns, as we shall discuss later. Overall, hinterland migration represents strong flows of people in both directions as is typical of migration streams in general.

The second pattern in the out-migration model is also the reciprocal of the in-migration pattern: intraurban migration. With the exception of the West Coast cities (to be described below), the intraurban component of Cleveland's out-migration field is very similar to that of its in-migration field (Figure 6). Such symmetry is characteristic of the in- and out-migration fields of most U.S. urban areas and simply illustrates that large numbers of migrants flow through every size of settlement within the system of urban places. As in the case of the in-migration fields, the intraurban part of out-migration fields can be explained partly by the size/distance relationship (the gravity model).

The third major pattern found in out-migration fields is accounted for by movement to recreation/amenity areas. Such flows can be fairly stable over time, but somewhat less so than the first two patterns. The relatively unstable flows extend to whatever scenic, warm weather, or recreation area that happens to be in favor at the time. Stable destinations include California, Arizona, and Florida, which show up consistently in Cleveland's out-migration fields in both 1955-1960 and 1965-

[20] With the proliferation of cable television installations in small and medium-sized towns, some large city television stations are widely seen much beyond their usual broadcast limits.

1970 (Figure 6), as they do in the fields of virtually every metropolitan area east of the Rockies and north of the Florida border. The flows to Arizona and Florida, in particular, are composed of many retirees seeking a warm weather environment. Recently other recreation/amenity areas have been appearing in metropolitan out-migration fields; for example, northern Michigan receives an influx of migrants from Detroit, parts of New England from New York, the Ozark region in Missouri and Arkansas from Chicago, and parts of Oregon from Los Angeles. The choice process of migrants making up these streams is influenced by: 1) interpersonal ties—retirees, for example, choose a retirement community to be with friends from their own home town; 2) advertising—metropolitan area newspapers frequently carry prominent ads for retirement and investment communities; and 3) vacation travel—individuals often decide where to move on the basis of first-hand, perhaps yearly, exposure to certain recreation/amenity areas.

As in the case of in-migration fields, the first three patterns nicely characterize most metropolitan out-migration; yet some additional patterns are observable in some fields. Again there are those which result from industrial and military transfers. There are also patterns resulting from *return migration* to nonmetropolitan areas which are sources of channelized migration streams and which are based on the friend and family ties between the two places. Many cities of the Northeast, Midwest, and California have a large "counterstream," composed of persons who return "home" to the nonmetropolitan place periodically (perhaps migrating back and forth as economic and job market conditions change in either or both locations). Others return "home" permanently dissatisfied with or unable to adjust to the city. Although it is just short of the minimum value and therefore does not show up on our map (Figure 6), there were 1509 migrants moving from Cleveland to the area in West Virginia in 1965-1970 that we previously identified as a source of a channelized flow. Return migration is another example of the symmetry that is typical of many migration streams.

Net Migration Fields

If the total in-migration to a place is compared to its total out-migration, a net migration figure results—the net effect of two separate migration streams. Similarly, the net effect of in- and out-migration fields can be described by the *net migration field*, derived by subtracting the out-migration stream from the place in question to each other place from the corresponding in-migration stream. In the map of the Cleveland net migration field (Figure 8), all other SEA's that contributed to a net loss or a net gain of at least 1000 migrants at Cleveland, 1955-1960, are indicated. This gives a picture of the areas that contributed to the growth of Cleveland and the areas which contributed to its decline.

The map shows that the migration streams to the amenity/recreation regions of California, Arizona, and Florida have much smaller counterstreams and thus contribute to the loss of population at Cleveland. On the

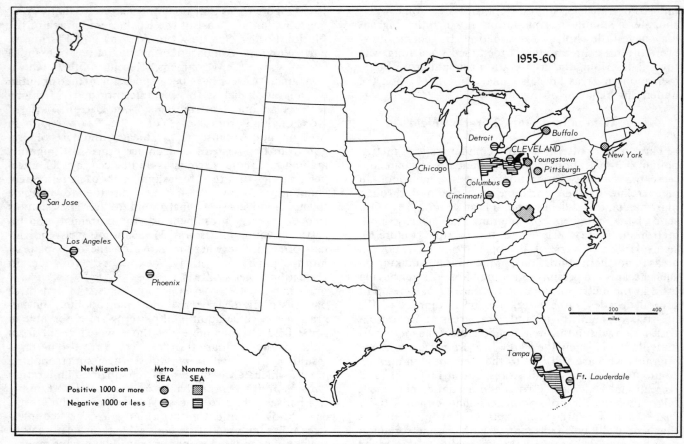

Figure 8. Net migration field of the Cleveland, Ohio SEA, 1955-1960. Source: U.S. Bureau of the Census (1967).

other hand, the channelized streams to and from southern West Virginia resulted in a gain of people to Cleveland, a long-standing tendency. Flows to and from urban areas in the Midwest and Northeast are mixed in their net effect on Cleveland's population, and losses to nearby nonmetropolitan areas were the rule.

Generally, net migration fields are not as stable through time as in- or out-migration fields because net figures tend to be small compared to gross flows. Nevertheless, net migration fields do reflect overall population redistribution trends—in Cleveland's field, for example, movements to California are clearly reflected. They also allow some understanding of the unique roles that might be played by different urban places as redistributors of population. Whereas most urban places have similar in- and out-migration fields and only a few prominent places in their net migration fields, others, such as Tuscaloosa, Alabama, have an imbalance that results in peculiar net migration patterns. Its net migration field shows population gains from every other SEA within

the state of Alabama and loss to numerous SEA's, especially metropolitan ones, all over the eastern U.S. Tuscaloosa is a college community attracting students largely from within the state (and college students are counted by the Census Bureau at their college residential location) but tending to redistribute people (including graduates) to a much broader area.

In the remainder of the paper we will make use of the ideas of in-, out-, and net migration fields when discussing migration trends, past, present, and future. They represent three ways to interpret geographically movements that contribute to the population gains or losses of different kinds of places.[21]

[21] Students are encouraged to consult the census volume "Migration between State Economic Areas" for 1955-1960 and 1965-1970 (U.S. Bureau of the Census, 1967, 1972). It is a simple task to construct the in- and out- and net migration fields for their home State Economic Areas, and to use them to speculate upon the nature and history of migration streams that are important to that place. A map of all the SEA's in the U.S. and a list of counties that each encompasses are included in each volume.

VI. MIGRATION PATTERNS BEFORE 1

The overall pattern of population movements in the 1950's and early 1960's was a culmination of some fundamental trends that had been evolving for several previous decades. The longest standing of these is the movement from nonmetropolitan to metropolitan places. As is the case in most countries of the world, "development" has coincided with lessening demand for farm labor and expanding employment in cities. As a consequence, the in-migration from the hinterlands of most cities exceeded the out-migration, as cities drew people from the region they commanded.

In association with this trend was the tendency for population to move up the urban size hierarchy. A popular hypothesis, the "step-wise migration" hypothesis, held that migration behavior led individuals off the farm, to a nearby town, on to a large regional center, and then perhaps to a very large city. Such behavior is rare for individuals, but often took place over a generation or two within one family. In any case there was net movement from smaller to larger places, as growth and agglomeration of industry in larger cities increased jobs there. The largest cities had the fastest growth rate, smaller cities a lesser growth rate, and small towns and villages a decline. Through the first half of this century, the net migration fields of a large city usually showed gains from many smaller cities, whereas those of the smaller cities showed losses to larger ones. It is important to note that there have been, throughout this century and the last, large flows in both directions among urban areas, the relatively smaller net figures redirecting the aggregate population to the larger places.

Broad regional patterns persisted through the 1950's as well. Notable is the considerable net migration of both blacks and whites from the South to northern and western cities. It accelerated rapidly among blacks between 1910 and 1920 as racial and economic problems surfaced in the South, and northern industry experienced increased demands for labor, especially during World War I. Catalysts to such movements included the recruiting of blacks by northern industry representatives, and by media campaigns, especially through the "national edition" of the *Chicago Defender* (Henri, 1975). The movement of whites from the South did not start as dramatically, but was equally important. Similar "pull" factors in the North and West brought whites out of agriculture from all over the South, and out of mining areas, particularly in Appalachia. In all cases, the channelized flow of information, often following railroad lines, the major transportation mode of the early twentieth century, was very important to the choice of a specific destination.

Large movements to the West Coast began when the droughts of the 1930's devastated agriculture in the Great Plains, stimulating migrants to seek jobs in California. Such movements continued after World War II, with origins expanding to the entire Midwest and much of the East. Similar although more gradual movements were depleting the population of other depressed areas, including northern Michigan, Wisconsin, and northern New England. Superimposed upon these relatively long-term trends, important flows from the Northeast and Midwest to Florida began to accelerate after World War II. Composed partly of retirees, these flows came to be very important in the overall migration patterns in the 1950's, and were reflected clearly in metropolitan migration fields during that time.

One result of the large net migration from rural areas was the depletion of the population in the most mobile age cohorts (young adult). This led to considerable aging of the population and to a natural decrease in many rural areas in the Plains States and the South. It also resulted in less out-migration after the middle 1950's because most of the persons likely to migrate had already done so. The out-migration trend had clearly peaked in the 1950's.

At the local scale, suburbanization from central cities, a slow but steady trend for decades, accelerated after World War II as urban areas embarked on the "freeway era." In the 1950's this resulted in an increasing differentiation between suburban rings and central cities in terms of jobs—commuting to and from the central city became a mass phenomenon—and in terms of racial and economic characteristics of the population as the poor and minorities had fewer opportunities to suburbanize. Gradually, jobs suburbanized too, so that by the early 1960's both manufacturing and sales/service jobs were highly dispersed throughout metropolitan areas instead of concentrated at the core as was typical earlier. Viewing this at the national scale, agglomeration and concentration of people and jobs into metropolitan areas was the rule; at the local scale there was concomitant dispersal within metropolitan areas.[22]

This brief sketch of pre-1965 migration trends provides the foundation upon which we will examine recent population redistribution patterns. Many of the recent changes have roots in earlier times, but seem to have been first observable in the middle 1960's. We will begin by considering locational preferences that were held by Americans at this critical time, the late 1960's.

---

[22] See Muller (1976) for more detail on the suburbanization process and its geographical consequences.

VII. RECENT MIGRATION PATTERNS

Location Preferences

Since the late 1960's social scientists have shown considerable interest in measuring the residential locational preferences of Americans. Several large national surveys have been conducted asking people to designate a preference for living in different types of places (e.g., large city, suburban area, small town, rural area). Others asked for broad regional preferences (e.g., the West, the South).

Fuguitt and Zuiches' (1975: 493) summary of several studies indicates an aggregate preference for "small cities and towns, and rural areas" ranging from a low of forty-nine percent of those surveyed to a high of seventy-nine percent. In spite of some difficulty in comparing studies because of the varied terminology used in assessing preferences (e.g., "rural" versus "farm"), there seemed to be a consensus that suggests a majority preference for areas that previous to the late 1960's had generally been losing population through migration. We do not know if such preferences are really just a recent phenomenon or have existed for a long time because there is but scanty evidence on locational preferences before 1966. If the preference structure has changed, these results could be a harbinger of subsequent changes in actual migration patterns. But such changes would be contingent upon the actual ability of persons to act upon their preferences. An ability *to move* is one of the prerequisites, and relative freedom of destination choice is another.

Further details of Fuguitt and Zuiches' study clarify the nature of locational preferences; whereas twenty percent of the persons sampled lived in cities larger than 500,000 population, only nine percent preferred such places; and of the twenty-four percent living in cities of 50,000 to 500,000 population, only sixteen percent preferred that size of place. In general, the 1481 persons surveyed preferred to live in smaller places than their residence at the time, a finding similar to those of other studies. This study, however, was different from others in an important respect.[23] It distinguished between rural and small/medium-sized towns within thirty miles of a large city and those farther away, and found that fifty-five percent of the sample preferred the locations accessible to urban areas and only nineteen percent the more remote locations. This finding discounts the implications of some other studies that people would fill up isolated rural areas of the country, particularly in the West, the most popularly preferred region. Fuguitt and Zuiches (1975: 496) conclude that:

> Many people respond positively to the idea of rural living, but not where it would entail disengagement from

[23] This distinction is important because most studies lumped together all small towns/rural areas without regard to any locational considerations. Other studies dealt with regional breakdowns of preferences, but used regions too large to assess accurately the type of environment preferred (the "West" included both Wolf Point, Montana and Los Angeles, California, two rather different living environments).

the metropolitan complex. This suggests a clear desire to have the best of both environments—which may include proximity to metropolitan employment, services, schools and facilities, along with the advantages of the smaller local-residential community for familial and neighborhood activities.

Their results clearly suggest the potential dominance of exurban growth and exurban migration in nonmetropolitan population changes. Further interpretations by Beale (1975) of the Fuguitt and Zuiches findings, however, suggest that migration from metropolitan to isolated nonmetropolitan places might stem from the preferences. Beale (1975: 12) states, "By a wide margin (65 percent to 35 percent), the big city people who preferred a nearby rural or small town residence ranked a more remote rural or small town place as their second choice, and thus as preferable to a big city."

Beale (1975: 13) goes on to suggest that migration since 1970 reflects "to a considerable extent" many people actually acting on the preference for a rural or small town environment over a metropolitan residence. The next sections review some of the migration trends in the late 1960's and early 1970's, contrast them to previous patterns, and document some of the many reasons for recent patterns.

Metropolitan and Nonmetropolitan Population Changes

Table 1 shows how the growth rates of metropolitan and nonmetropolitan areas have changed in recent years. Standardized to an average annual growth rate, the data show that metropolitan areas in 1970-1975 have been growing at a much slower rate than in the previous decade, and central cities of metropolitan areas have been losing population in the more recent period. Suburban areas outside of central cities were still growing at a 1.8 percent per year rate but that was down from a 2.4 percent rate previously. A substantial increased growth rate, however, was observed in nonmetropolitan places.

The growth rate decline in central cities is a contin-

TABLE 1. PERCENT POPULATION CHANGE, SMSA's AND NONMETROPOLITAN AREAS, 1960–1970 AND 1970–1975

	Average Annual Percent Change	
	1960 to 1970	1970 to 1975
Metropolitan Areas	1.5	0.7
(in central cities)	(0.6)	(−0.6)
(outside central cities)	(2.4)	(1.8)
Nonmetropolitan Areas	0.7	1.2

Source: U.S. Bureau of the Census (1976).

uation of the decentralization trend within metropolitan areas (SMSA's). Fifteen of the twenty-one largest U.S. central cities (those having 500,000 or more population) lost population between 1960 and 1970—such losses were continuing in the 1970's (Morrison and Wheeler, 1976). In the 1970's, not only are central cities in general losing population but so are entire metropolitan areas; whereas only one of the twenty-five largest metropolitan areas (Pittsburgh) lost population between 1960 and 1970, ten lost population between 1970 and 1975. Further, at least forty-four of all 259 SMSA's were losing population (Morrison and Wheeler, 1976). Thus we can see a general reversal in growth patterns—with non-metropolitan places having increasing growth rates and metropolitan places decreasing growth rates. Similar trends have been observed, and perhaps even preceded those in the U.S., in several countries in Western Europe and in Japan (Sundquist, 1975; Vining and Kontuly, 1976).

What is the role of migration in this reversal? Table 2 shows that, in the 1965-1970 period, metropolitan areas as a whole were net receivers of migrants, but they were experiencing considerable net out-migration (over 1.5 million) in the first half of the 1970 decade. The net exchange of people between metropolitan and non-metropolitan places had reversed itself. Partly respon-

TABLE 2. MIGRATION TO AND FROM SMSA's 1965–1970 AND 1970–1975

	1965–1970	1970–1975
Net Migration	+352,133	−1,594,000
In-migration	+5,809,415	+5,127,000
Out-migration	−5,457,282	−6,721,000

Source: U.S. Bureau of the Census (1975b).

sible for this was some decrease in the total migration stream into metropolitan areas (about 700,000)—but the larger component causing the net reversal was the 1.3 million *increase* in out-migration from metropolitan areas (not just central cities) which has led to a big part of the change in growth rates seen in Table 1.

Spatial Patterns of Net Migration

The reversal has meant renewed growth of many non-metropolitan places which, for decades, had been declining as a direct or indirect result of large out-migrations. Beale and Fuguitt (1975) compiled the map in Figure 9 by aggregating net migration data for 2470 non-metropolitan counties in twenty-six regions. It shows,

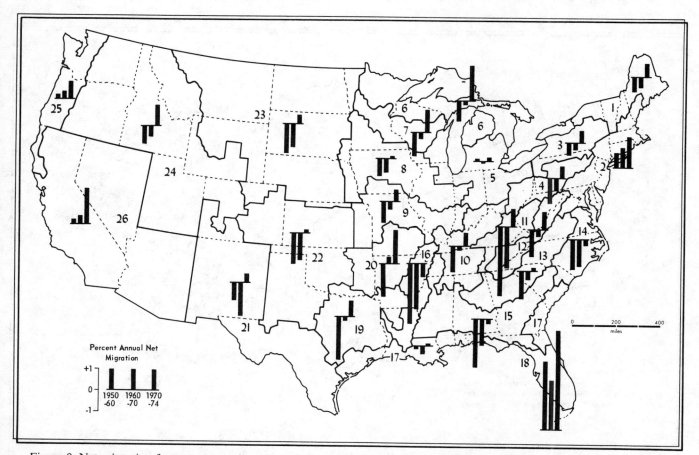

Figure 9. Net migration for nonmetropolitan counties in twenty-six regions, 1950-1960, 1960-1970, and 1970-1973. See Beale and Fuguitt (1975: 3) for data sources used in compiling this map. Source: redrawn from Beale and Fuguitt (1975: Map 3, p. 30) with permission of the Center for Demography and Ecology, University of Wisconsin-Madison.

for most nonmetropolitan places, the rather dramatic changes in net migration, from net losses of population through migration in 1950-1960 and 1960-1970 periods to a net gain in 1970-1973. These reversals were experienced in nonmetropolitan areas of New England and the Northeast (regions No. 1 and No. 3), northern Wisconsin, Minnesota, and Michigan (6 and 7), many areas in the South (especially 10, 12, 19, and 20) and the Plains and Interior West (21, 22, 23, and 24). Hence the reversal was hardly limited to one type of nonmetropolitan place nor to one region.

Continued growth through migration, rather than a reversal, is observable on the West Coast and in Florida (25, 26, and 18) which have been attracting migrants from colder climatic areas of the U.S. for some time, and in the Megalopolis region (2) which is highly urbanized and has been experiencing exurban growth or "spillover" from metropolitan areas through the last three decades. The major exception to the tendency for net in-migration in 1970-1973 was region 16, a lower Mississippi Valley area with a traditional cotton plantation economy and a black population majority. Even here, however, the decrease in net out-migration was sufficient to influence the region to start growing in population after several decades of decline (Morrison and Wheeler, 1976: 16).

A more detailed spatial picture of the results of these

migration reversals can be seen in Figure 10. To construct this map, Census Bureau estimates of net migration by county for 1970-1974 were consulted.[24] Because individual county estimates are sometimes subject to question, and because description of broad patterns is sought, the map shows regions defined as aggregates of at least three contiguous counties which experienced a net in-migration during 1970-1974 exceeding by at least five percent the 1970 county population. The map, therefore, shows regions of relative growth from migration, rather than that for individual counties. It is biased somewhat toward small (typically nonurban) counties because in such places rather small net in-migration figures can exceed five percent of the population—none-

[24] For each year since 1970, the Census Bureau has had a cooperative project with local and state agencies to compile annual data on total population, births, deaths, and net migration. They are published by the Bureau in *Current Population Reports,* Series P-25 and P-26, one issue for each state (see U.S.Bureau of the Census, 1975a). These reports are available at most university and college libraries, and at many public libraries. The estimates are computed from local birth and death records, Medicare statistics, records of movement of military and other institutional populations, and federal income tax records, among other sources. The estimates for any one given county are rounded to the nearest 100 people and are subject to fallibility. Nonetheless, they are the best available migration data at the county level and, because they are up-dated annually, give a general dynamic picture of population changes resulting from migration (as well as other components.).

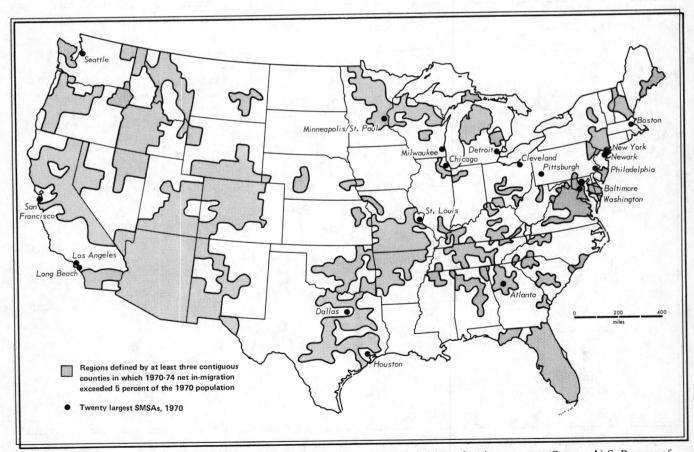

Figure 10. Regions of relative growth due to migration, 1970-1974. For definition of regions see text. Source: U.S. Bureau of the Census, 1975a.

theless, it shows those places, rural and urban, where the *relative* impact upon the population because of migration has been substantial.

The growth areas shown here correspond to some extent to the broader-scale patterns seen on Figure 9; both metropolitan and nonmetropolitan Arizona and Florida stand out, the Interior West has considerable nonmetropolitan growth, and northern Minnesota/Wisconsin/Michigan and the Ozark region of Missouri and Arkansas are large contiguous regions of nonmetropolitan growth. Also numerous smaller regions of growth are scattered throughout the Interior South, Megalopolis, and New England.

Nonmetropolitan areas near large cities tend to appear on this map as well. With the exceptions of Milwaukee, Cleveland, and Pittsburgh (where there are single adjacent counties meeting the growth criterion), there are growth regions neighboring all of the twenty largest SMSA's, probably the result of exurban migration. There are many areas, however, which did not meet the mapping criterion—much of the Great Plains, a band from the Corn Belt to Pennsylvania and New York and considerable areas in the South. Also, most central cities and other counties within metropolitan areas do not meet the criterion, although many suburban counties are still experiencing net in-migration, but not above the five percent criterion.

Characteristics of Growing and Declining Places

Before considering migration streams and migration behavior that underlie the net migration patterns shown on Figures 9 and 10, we will consider briefly the types of places which are attracting large numbers of migrants and those which are not.

Several attributes of places relate to their recent attractiveness to migrants. One of the most important is the recreation and retirement character of many places—Arizona and Florida, of course, but also Oregon, the northern Midwest, New England, and numerous places in the South outside of Florida. Retirement communities often coincide with recreation areas, which in turn are oriented toward reservoirs and other bodies of water, and toward hilly, scenic environments. The existence of recreation or retirement activities creates jobs in the service sector, thus attracting job-seeking migrants of all ages and tending to retain local populations which might otherwise out-migrate.

The ability to attract industry is a second critically important characteristic of places that grow through migration. Having shown a decentralization trend prior to 1970, industry was then and is after 1970 contributing to the revival of many nonmetropolitan areas in a wide variety of dispersed locations (Beale, 1975: 9). Part of the basis for the decentralization is the preference for amenity/recreation regions by individual or small groups of decision-makers who choose places for small factories or branch plants. In the South, for example, many growing nonmetropolitan places are in recreation areas and at the same time are attracting industry.[25]

Another set of places growing as a result of migration, a set that is nearly mutually exclusive of recreation/retirement areas (Beale, 1975), has large colleges or universities, especially those that are state supported. Other institution-dominated counties show growth, too, including some with military populations, state capitals, and other federal and state employment bases. These are dispersed throughout the country and typically do not show up on Figure 10.

A majority of the places growing rapidly through migration, however, are those which are not characterized by type, but instead simply by location near metropolitan areas. According to Beale (1975: 7) about five-eighths of the total net in-migration to nonmetropolitan counties between 1970 and 1973 was experienced in those nonmetropolitan counties which are adjacent to metropolitan areas. There are some recreation/amenity places and places attractive to industry near metropolitan areas that draw exurban migrants; but there is also considerable exurban growth in places that can be characterized only by their location.

Those areas not attracting large numbers of migrants include broad areas which have stable, prosperous farming economies, including much of the Great Plains and Corn Belt. They neither have attracted industry in large amounts nor possess the recreation and amenity attractions that might lure retirees and other migrants, but they continue to be economically viable. There are exceptions; isolated counties in Kansas, Iowa, and Indiana, for example, have experienced surprising recent in-migration.

Also not yet attracting a large positive net in-migration are the rural counties in the South with large black populations. For one thing, they tend to be in areas of the South that have been by-passed by major reservoir projects and developers of retirement communities. Also, industrial location decision-makers tend to avoid predominantly black counties on the basis that they perceive blacks as less qualified workers and as having a greater propensity to unionize. Return migration of blacks to the South has not increased sufficiently to cause major population reversals, although out-migration has decreased enough to slow population declines considerably.

---

[25] This correspondence of places with recreation and industry is reinforced by the fact that relatively cheap power is available to industry in association with reservoirs that are located in hilly, scenic recreation areas. These also happen to be the places in the South that were dominantly settled by whites, and today have dominantly white populations.

VIII. DECISIONS UNDERLYING RECENT MIGRATION PATTERNS

The reversal of migration streams which now carry more people from metropolitan to nonmetropolitan places can be explained partially by separating the decision to move from the decision of where to move. For at least two reasons more and more people are now making the decision to move from metropolitan areas. First, a rapidly expanding proportion of the U.S. population is in the over sixty-four age cohort and, as retirement ages decline in many occupation categories (from the traditional sixty-five down to sixty-two, sixty, or even fifty-five), an even more rapidly increasing proportion of the population is retired. Thus an increasing number and proportion of people are now free from job ties that would keep them in a place and are able to make a total displacement migration decision.

Typical retirees are also on substantially greater incomes than their counterparts of twenty or thirty years ago. By the late 1960's and early 1970's, Social Security and other retirement programs were providing steady incomes to a much greater proportion of the retired population than previously—hence, many more persons at that stage of the life cycle have the financial ability to make the decision to move. Coupled with this is that the cost of living was inflating rapidly during the early 1970's, particularly in metropolitan areas, creating an additional stimulus for persons on fixed incomes to move away from such places.

Second, as the popular press increases its coverage and commentary of urban problems of crime, safety, transportation, and fiscal affairs, not only in central cities but elsewhere within metropolitan areas, the overall middle-class and upper-middle-class image of urban and suburban life has been modified. Coupled with this is the mass media dramatization of the rural, backwoods, and small-town environments as desirable. For many, especially white middle- and upper-middle-income whites, the relative place utility of living in an urban area has reached the doubtful level and the decision to move out is contemplated. In addition to these two broad factors, there are those who have little choice about moving and are transferred with industrial movements and hence "decentralized."

The question now becomes: where to move? This will be discussed in terms of different types of migration streams: 1) exurban, 2) migration to more isolated nonmetropolitan places, and 3) migration down the urban hierarchy.

Exurban Migration Streams

The greatest change in nonmetropolitan America is perhaps taking place near metropolitan places in small towns and rural areas that may have been stable or declining for decades. Exurban migration is responsible for much of the change in these places. Figure 11 and Table 3 show the nature of exurban migration in the Atlanta area by comparing migration between the five county metropolitan area and four surrounding nonmetropolitan SEA's, 1955-1960 and 1965-1970. The nonmetropolitan SEA's are clearly beyond the traditional tract development suburban areas immediately surrounding Atlanta (Figure 11). Atlanta gained population from each in 1955-1960 (Table 3) consistent with the draw most cities had upon their hinterlands for migrants during the period, but lost to each in 1965-1970. Particularly large net losses (6093 and 4408) from Atlanta in the latter period were to areas 3 and 4, the ones immediately adjacent to the boundaries of the metropolitan area. The most important change in migration streams accounting for the reversal with respect to these areas was the near doubling of migration *from* Atlanta (8240 to 15,134 and 11,727 to 21,220). At the same time Atlanta's draw upon migrants from these two SEA's remained about the same. The growth of these areas through migration, then, was clearly the result of a considerable increase in exurban migration from Atlanta, a tendency that has probably persisted, if not increased, since 1970.

Migration from Atlanta accounted for approximately twenty-eight percent of all in-migration to area 3 in 1965-1970 and approximately thirty-eight percent of all in-migrants to area 4—an indication of the influence of Atlanta upon the population of these areas. It is likely that exurban growth surrounding Atlanta (as well as other metropolitan areas) is a product of both exurban migrants and migrants from other metropolitan areas who chose an exurban location near Atlanta. The migration flows discussed with reference to the Atlanta area are typical of most metropolitan regions in the U.S.

One by-product of exurban migration is the recent growth of many small towns and villages. In Kansas, for instance (Figure 12), villages of population less than 1000 in either 1950 or 1970 which at least doubled their populations between the two dates are, without exception, located in exurban areas of Wichita, Topeka, and Kansas City, the three major metropolitan areas of the state. Virtually none of the other villages near the three metropolitan places were declining in population. Elsewhere in the state some villages grew and more declined through a variety of factors (Groop, 1976), but a substantial part of village growth in Kansas is related to proximity to urban places.

The decision to move for exurban migrants may relate to a wide variety of factors, including dissatisfaction with city or suburban living environments. But the decision where to move very likely relates to a need or desire to have some ties to the urban place; direct ties to a job on the urban fringe; desire to have regular access to shopping or entertainment activities on the fringe; or simply contact through the mass media. These ties are coupled with a nonurban living environment in the choice of a destination.

Figure 11. The Atlanta, Georgia metropolitan SEA and surrounding nonmetropolitan SEA's.

Migration to More Isolated Nonmetropolitan Places

Many persons choosing to leave a metropolitan area for a nonmetropolitan place beyond exurban range do so on the basis of either previous residential locations or vacation experiences. For example, a retiree who has spent decades in a metropolitan place after having been raised in a rural area, attains the freedom to move upon retirement, then chooses to go "back home." The most feasible place in the search space is that place where the retiree grew up and with which fairly consistent ties have been maintained through the years. Most large metropolitan areas have rapidly expanding populations of rural-born persons now retiring who might make such decisions. The result could be significant reversals of hinterland migration and return migration streams complementing channelized flows. As yet, return migration has not played a major role in the population reversal of nonmetropolitan places in the South (Long and Hansen, 1975), but is observable in some places and is likely to play a greater role in the near future as the rural-born retiree and previous channelized flows are reversed.

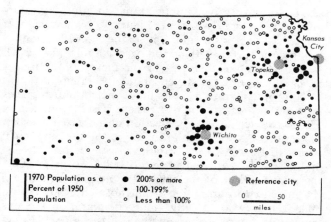

Figure 12. Village population growth, Kansas, 1950-1970. Source: Groop (1975: Figure 16, p. 80). Redrawn by permission of Richard E. Groop.

More important in the nonmetropolitan reversal, in general, is the creation of relatively new migration streams, rather than the reversal of the old. Again consider the metropolitan retiree making the decision to move and thinking about where to go—the most feasible possibility may be that place where he or she had been vacationing annually. Perhaps investment had already been made in a second home, a cottage, or land in the vacation area, a factor which would bind the location decision. In any case, new migration streams follow previous vacation pathways. Migration streams created by such a process can be somewhat channelized, just as vacation trips are channelized—individuals from a particular town or city going to a common vacation area, the area having been advertised by word of mouth. Mass media advertisements of vacation areas and retirement developments, too, are often concentrated upon particular metropolitan areas, stimulating a channelized flow.

Nonretirees moving to recreation areas may also be influenced by previous vacation or residential experiences, but the economic and job attractions at the alternative destination may induce many of them to broaden their search spaces. This is another way in which new migration streams are created—flows to areas where jobs are available.

The migration reversal in the nonmetropolitan Interior West is an illustration of the creation of new migration streams. Most of the eighteen nonmetropolitan SEA's in the states of Montana, Idaho, Wyoming, Utah,

TABLE 3. MIGRATION BETWEEN THE ATLANTA SEA AND NEIGHBORING NONMETROPOLITAN SEA's, 1955–1960 AND 1965–1970

Nonmetropolitan SEA	From Atlanta		To Atlanta		Atlanta Net	
	1955–60	1965–70	1955–60	1965–70	1955–60	1965–70
Georgia 1	3,207	5,000	6,212	4,895	+3,005	−105
Georgia 2	1,664	2,560	3,078	2,279	+1,414	−281
Georgia 3	8,240	15,134	9,560	9,041	+1,320	−6,093
Georgia 4	11,727	21,220	15,208	16,812	+3,481	−4,408

Source: U.S. Bureau of the Census (1967, 1972).

and Colorado received important net in-migrations during the 1970 to 1974 period (Figure 10). The area as a whole had been losing migrants in the 1955-1960 period, but by the 1965-1970 period was gaining (Table 4). Migration out of this area to the metropolitan places *within* the five states stayed about the same, just over 81,000; but migration from those metropolitan places into the nonmetropolitan areas increased from nearly 53,000 to over 71,000, a reflection of increased exurban migration. Although migration out of the nonurban places to thirty-two major cities elsewhere in the West and Midwest increased from 120,000 to over 137,000, the major source of the reversal in new migration was the increased in-migration from those cities (72,000 to 300,000). New or greatly enlarged migration streams from outside the region emerged in the 1965-1970 period, no doubt a result partly of the previous vacation experiences of persons making up these streams, and partly of recent energy-related developments in the Interior West.

The net migration fields of Los Angeles, 1955–1960 and 1965–1970 (Figure 13), served also to illustrate some points about changing migration streams that affect growing nonmetropolitan areas. As expected, Los Angeles gained large numbers of migrants from large eastern and midwestern cities in 1955-1960, but lost to several other SEA's in California, both metropolitan and nonmetropolitan. In the period Los Angeles was, in effect, a net receiver of migrants from the nation and a redistributor of people to other places in California. By 1965-1970 the number of urban places in the Midwest and East from which Los Angeles made major gains was reduced from seven to five, a reflection of the general slowdown in migration to California by that time. Although Los Angeles continued as a redistributor to California, it also lost large numbers of migrants to Oregon and Seattle (from which it had previously gained). This is a reflection of the attraction of the Pacific Northwest first as a vacation place for southern Californians and subsequently as an attraction for southern California migrants. A similar phenomenon applies to recent intensified migration from southern California to the Sierra Nevada foothills of central and northern California. In the Oregon case, the increasing streams of southern California migrants have caused considerable concern among Oregon residents fearing environmental degradation that might be associated with rapid growth through massive in-migration. Oregon residents do not want their state to turn into another "southern California"—one possible outcome of large migration to any amenity/recreation area.

Migration field changes in the South, including the appearance of new migration streams, have been observed as well. The net migration fields of three SEA's in the South are used as contrasting examples. Arkansas SEA Number 9, an area in the Ozark region with many tourist and retirement attractions and a nearly 100 percent white population, has been growing rapidly since 1970 as a result of migration. In 1955-1960 the area was still experiencing a net out-migration, but that reversed by 1965-1970 (Figure 14a).[26]

Its 1955-1960 net migration field showed net out-migration to adjacent areas in Arkansas (including the area just west of SEA 9, the home of the University of Arkansas at Fayetteville), and to the regional centers of Little Rock and Kansas City. But also in that period Arkansas SEA 9 was attracting a net in-migration from Chicago, a source of migrants who probably had had vacation experience rather than residential experience in the Ozarks. (Realtors in the area explain that the Chicago area is their biggest market for persons interested in land and home sales, rather than the closer metropolitan areas of St. Louis or Kansas City).

By 1965-1970 net migration from Chicago increased and the large net out-migrations to Kansas City and Little Rock disappeared, even though the net out-migration to the Fayetteville area still persisted, probably accounted for largely by college students. Also appearing is a net in-flow from Los Angeles, which likely includes some return migrants as Los Angeles was a common destination for earlier out-migrants.

[26] The area was, in fact, one of the early nonmetropolitan areas in the country that experienced a significant reversal of net migration (other than some exurban areas).

TABLE 4. MIGRATION BETWEEN NONMETROPOLITAN SEA's OF THE INTERIOR WEST AND SELECTED METROPOLITAN SEA's, 1955–1960 AND 1965–1970*

	To/From Metropolitan SEA's Within the Interior West		To/From 32 Metropolitan SEA's Outside of the Interior West	
	1955–1960	1965–1970	1955–1960	1965–1970
Out-migration from Nonmetropolitan SEA's	81,090	81,558	120,587	137,434
In-migration to Non-metropolitan SEA's	52,875	77,290	71,974	300,001
Net Migration	−28,215	−4,298	−48,613	+162,569

* For purposes of this table, the Interior West is defined as the states of Montana, Idaho, Wyoming, Colorado, and Utah.

Source: U.S. Bureau of the Census (1967, 1972).

Figure 13. Net migration fields of Los Angeles, California, 1955-1960 and 1965-1970. Source: U.S. Bureau of the Census (1967, 1972).

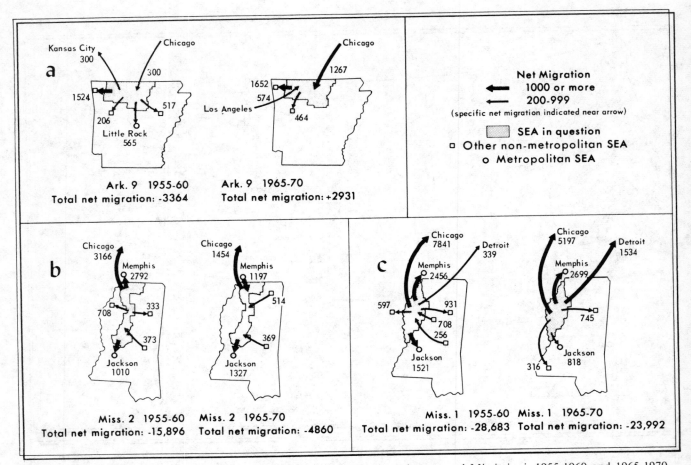

Figure 14. Net migration fields of three nonmetropolitan SEA's in Arkansas and Mississippi, 1955-1960 and 1965-1970. Source: U.S. Bureau of the Census (1967, 1972).

Another place in the South which experienced a turn-around and has been gaining migrants since 1970 is Mississippi SEA 2, a place with a majority black population (51.4 percent black in 1970) (Figure 14b). Large net flows in 1955-1960 included a channelized stream to Chicago and losses to the regional centers of Memphis and Jackson. The Jackson flow persisted in 1965-1970 but the channelized flow was halved and, most importantly, the area experienced a turn-around with respect to Memphis. The northern part of this SEA borders on Tennessee and the exurban migration from Memphis was sufficient in this part of the SEA to reduce significantly the net out-migration of the entire SEA.[27] It also was probably a major contributor to the subsequent migration turn-around in the 1970's. Thus the area has been a beneficiary of a good location—one near enough to a metropolitan place to profit from its exurban migration.

In contrast to the migration fields of Arkansas 9 and Mississippi 2 is that of Mississippi 1 (Figure 14c), an area that has a largely black population (60.3 percent in 1970) and which in 1970-1974 was still experiencing net

out-migration. Here channelized flows to Chicago and Detroit have persisted during the two time periods, as did flows to the regional centers of Jackson and Memphis. The area experienced no reversals of major migration streams and no new streams were created—hence considerable net out-migration was still the rule in 1965-1970, although less than in the previous time period.

Arkansas 9 and Mississippi 1 and 2 are just examples, but the dynamics of their migration fields illustrate important trends. In the South, in general, most largely white counties as well as some majority black counties experienced reversals because of their locations near large cities—and net migration to these cities showed distinct reversals. Others had some channelized flows persisting with some newly created streams from major cities within or outside of the region. A few others had clear return flows. In any case, those places in the South which are experiencing significant net in-migrations have in the past experienced distinct observable changes in their migration fields.

Migration Down the Urban Hierarchy

The third important type of migration trend concerns migration among metropolitan areas. By the 1940's and 1950's the majority of total nonlocal migration by the

---

[27] This illustrates a weakness of using SEA migration data. There can be important variations in migration rates of character of migration flows from place to place within SEA's, especially large SEA's. These variations are hidden by aggregate total figures for the SEA.

white population of the U.S. was *among* metropolitan areas. By the late 1950's this was true for black migration as well (Tilly, 1968). In both cases, the long-term migration *to* metropolitan areas had been exceeded by movement between them because of the depletion of nonmetropolitan population numbers and the great increase in proportion of the population (and hence potential migrants) in the metropolitan areas. Prior to the middle 1960's, the tendency was for the net exchange of urban migrants to be toward successively larger metropolitan places.

More recently, the tendency is for a net exchange down the urban size hierarchy. This can be observed at the national scale; the largest metropolitan areas such as New York and Chicago typically are losing population to such smaller metropolitan places in various regions as Kansas City, Philadelphia, Minneapolis/St. Paul, and Atlanta. There are major exceptions to this trend, but there has been an increase in observable cases of such net exchanges. This is also the tendency at the regional scale, as many major cities now lose migrants to smaller metropolitan areas in their respective regions. Table 5 illustrates this for Chicago and its migration ties with the other six metropolitan SEA's within the state of Illinois, 1955-1960 and 1965-1970. Chicago was gaining from four of them in the earlier period, but lost to all but

one in 1965-1970. The reversals, although not large in terms of net migration, often represented fairly substantial percentage increases in the out-migration streams from Chicago. Migration from Chicago to Rockford, for example increased from 3337 to 4600 (an increase of over thirty-seven percent). Similarly, flows to Peoria went up from 3012 to 4851, and to Springfield from 1205 and 2405. The reverse flows to Chicago did not increase enough to prevent the reversal of net flows.

Reasons for this trend are not unlike those for other recent reversals in migration patterns. Industrial growth has been greater in small metropolitan areas than in large ones—a part of the overall decentralization of industry in the U.S. The perceived metropolitan "push" factor related to crime, fiscal problems, and so forth, is probably greater among residents of larger metropolitan areas—the response is often a move to a smaller metropolitan area. Smaller metropolitan areas represent alternatives where adequate employment opportunities are available. They, of course, have their own exurban environments that are possible destinations for persons moving down the urban hierarchy. Small towns and rural nonfarm places are growing around smaller metropolitan areas such as Peoria, Springfield, and Rockford, as well as around Topeka and Wichita, Kansas (Figure 12).

TABLE 5. MIGRATION BETWEEN THE CHICAGO SEA AND OTHER METROPOLITAN SEA's IN ILLINOIS, 1955–1960 AND 1965–1970

State Economic Area	1955–1960			1965–1970		
	To Chicago	From Chicago	Chicago net Gain (+) or Loss (−)	To Chicago	From Chicago	Chicago net Gain (+) or Loss (−)
Rock Island/Moline	1,663	1,691	− 98	1,801	1,713	+ 88
Rockford	2,383	3,337	+ 954	3,105	4,600	−1,495
Peoria	2,872	3,012	− 140	3,818	4,851	−1,033
Springfield	1,944	1,205	+ 739	1,819	2,405	− 586
E. St. Louis	2,707	1,551	+1,156	2,549	2,807	− 258
Decatur	1,251	971	+ 280	1,671	1,760	− 89

Source: U.S. Bureau of the Census (1967, 1972).

IX. REGIONAL CASE STUDIES

Case Studies Using Aggregate Migration Data

To illustrate many of the important migration concepts accounting for recent population changes, we will examine aggregate migration trends in two regions that are newly experiencing growth following decades of steady or declining population. First are the northern New England states of Vermont, New Hampshire, and Maine, whose population growth has, until recently,

been lagging behind that of the nation as a whole and whose rural areas have had depopulation through large out-migration streams typical of many relatively depressed rural areas in the U.S.[28] Net migration by county for 1960-1970, shown in Figure 15, is mapped on a per year basis and shows that most counties in Maine, plus several in northern Vermont and New Hampshire,

[28] See Lewis (1972) for a discussion of the population trends in the area during the twentieth century.

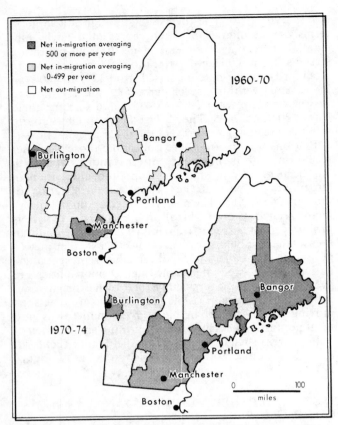

Figure 15. Annual net migration by county, Vermont, New Hampshire, and Maine, 1960-1970 and 1970-1974. Total net migration for the two time periods was divided by the number of years in the period to obtain the average net migration figure. Source: Bowles *et al.* (1975) and U.S. Bureau of the Census (1975a).

were still losing population through migration. This area of net out-migration had shrunk to a two county area by the 1970-1974 period. For the first time in many decades, almost all areas within the three states were experiencing net in-migration.

Major growth areas (those having a net in-migration of at least 500 persons per year) expanded considerably in two fairly distinct spatial patterns: a growth axis covering most of the state of New Hampshire, and an axis of growth along the Maine coast. Not coincidentally these two areas straddle two major interstate highways radiating from the Boston metropolitan area. There has been considerably improved access to Boston, and other major urban centers of the East, which in turn has enhanced exurban growth (evident in 1960-1970 in two counties in southern New Hampshire that had been growing partly because of tax advantages for industry in the state). There has been a boost to both the winter and summer tourist activities, which have provided new employment opportunities and have been the antecedent to later in-migration.

The various amenities of the Maine coast axis and the New Hampshire axis are the main attractions. With more and more retirees and others choosing to move to amenity areas, such areas in New England with the best accessibility were the first to feel the population growth.

Parts of northern New England (especially the skiing regions in central and southern Vermont and New Hampshire) are now actually populated by more people than census figures might have us believe. There are essentially three populations that share these locales: permanent year-round residents, winter residents who cluster near winter sport opportunities, and summer residents many of whom live in Boston or other parts of Megalopolis. We can be reasonably sure that the year-round residents are counted in census data, but the others may or may not be. The second home phenomenon has been particularly important to the growth of such areas within the region. More and more persons have been acquiring homes, usually for summer use as a retreat from the urban areas of the East—many of these, in turn, have been converted to year-round homes (or nearly so), as their owners retire or otherwise make the decision to move from an urban place. The improved interstate access has been a catalyst to this sector of population growth because many places were very difficult to reach in the winter. A similar phenomenon is observable for most of the rural hilly or mountainous margins of Megalopolis, as well as for numerous areas with good access to large population centers.

Additional factors important to the reversal in the region are not unlike those of most areas of non-metropolitan revival. They include recent growth of industry in relatively isolated places (e.g., Burlington, Vermont) and those with access to metropolitan places (e.g., southern New Hampshire), and some areas with educational institutions. Burlington has been attracting migrants for some time as a result of a combination of both of these factors.[29]

The second case study area is the state of Arkansas, a region which has been much less influenced by accessibility to large population centers. It was chosen because it includes both very rapidly growing places and areas of continuing decline—it is a microcosm, to a considerable extent, of the overall population change patterns in the entire South. In the 1960-1970 period, only six counties gained more than 500 persons per year through migration (Figure 16). These included the Fayetteville area in the northwest corner and the Little Rock area (homes of the major state university and state capital, respectively), and two counties elsewhere in the Ozark hill region in northern and western Arkansas. The area of migration loss covered the entire southern and eastern portions of the state. By 1970-1974, the major growth region had expanded and the loss region contracted.

Reasons for these changing spatial patterns are related to the contrasting character of the northwest and southeast parts of the state. The northern and western parts have been growing partly through the recreation/amenity lure of the Ozarks which for decades had been losing population, but had in the 1960's become one of the first such regions in the U.S. to show a migration reversal. Although not seen in Figure 15,

[29] Lewis (1972) discusses the major factors contributing to recent growth in northern New England, including accessibility, second homes, manufacturing, recreation, and educational institutions.

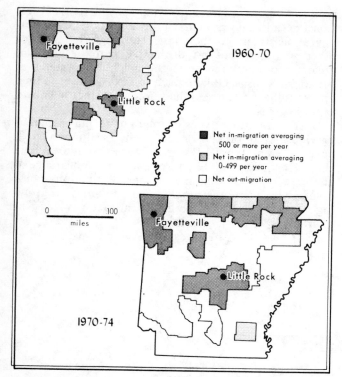

Figure 16. Annual net migration by county, Arkansas, 1960-1970 and 1970-1974. Data compilation and sources same as Figure 14.

virtually all of the counties in northwestern Arkansas drew a significant net in-migration of persons in the over sixty-four age cohort during the 1960's, while most were still experiencing net out-migration in other age cohorts (except a few university areas which had net in-migrations in the young adult cohorts) (Bowles *et al.*, 1975). Thus persons in the retirement stage of the life cycle were forerunners of the later migration turn-around for all age groups.

As we demonstrated earlier, new and return migration streams along with the decline of major out-migration streams have been the aggregate migration patterns affecting the area. Many retirees and others employed in service sector jobs have moved in, drawn in part by major reservoir projects and associated recreation developments across the northern part of the state, some dating back to the early 1950's. Industry has also enhanced the attraction to the area, especially near the Arkansas River navigation project. In short, all of the factors drawing migrants to relatively isolated nonmetropolitan areas discussed earlier come together in this region.

In southeast Arkansas the economy is still largely agricultural and the majority population is black. As in many black areas of the South with the traditional plantation economy and relatively few recreation/amenity developments, this area is not attracting new migrants or new migration streams, nor has the out-migration been reduced enough yet to create a migration reversal.

Migration to Harrison, Arkansas: A Case Study Using Individual Survey Data

In order to learn more about the decision-making process that takes migrants to relatively isolated places, this section reports briefly on the results of interviews with recent migrants to Harrison, Arkansas. During the summer of 1976, 210 persons who migrated into Harrison since 1970, identified through several methods including the Welcome Wagon representative and municipal water records, were asked about their reasons for moving, their search spaces, and their reasons for picking Harrison.[30]

Several characteristics of Harrison make it an excellent case study setting: it is located in the scenic Ozark region of northern Arkansas and is near numerous recreation facilities. With a 1975 population of about 9000, it has become a center for business and government activity in the northern part of the state, and has been attracting industry partly because industrial decision-makers are attracted to the amenities of the region.[31] Whereas Harrison is not exclusively a retirement community, as are several towns nearby, many retirees have settled there because it is one of the larger towns and has shopping and other desirable facilities. In effect, Harrison is a microcosm of the growing Ozark region and perhaps quite representative of the many nonmetropolitan places in the U.S. experiencing significant growth. As a consequence there is not just one type of migrant attracted to Harrison; instead, the several types contributing to the growth of the Ozarks and other nonmetropolitan places are all represented.

The 210 migrants came from twenty-eight different states, but the in-migration field was dominated by Arkansas (forty migrants), Illinois (twenty-four), California (twenty-three), Missouri (eighteen), Iowa (sixteen), and Texas (fourteen). Reasons for migrating confirm the idea that Harrison has a diversity of newcomers: job transfers accounted for forty-five (21.4 percent) of the migrants. These persons came with either one of the newly established industries in Harrison or with a state agency. Seventy-one (33.8 percent) were retirees choosing the Ozarks for amenities such as climate and Harrison in particular for its services. Ninety-four (44.8 percent) moved for other reasons—to look for a job, to establish a business, or to return to the place of birth.

These three categories—transferees, retirees, and others—contrast in terms of their locational decisions. Seventy-six percent of the transferees had no previous experience with the Ozark area. The other two groups had extensive experience to help in their locational decisions, including previous residence, vacation experience or having relatives there. About thirty percent of the retirees had lived there previously, the highest of the three groups, and another sixty percent had other experience with the Ozarks.

[30] The interviews and the analysis for this section were done by Fred M. Shelley, University of Illinois, whose help is gratefully acknowledged.
[31] Local Chamber of Commerce and municipal officials claim that many industries are turned away each year; in effect, Harrison picks the "cream of the crop."

As might be expected the search spaces contrasted—from the typical one-place search space of the transferee to a variety in the size and nature of the search spaces of the other groups. Retirees tended to search elsewhere within the Ozarks (partly corresponding to their vacation experiences), whereas other migrants had even more dispersed search spaces. These search processes are reflected in the aggregate in-migration on fields of each migrant group. Of job transferees, forty-two percent came from elsewhere in Arkansas (especially outside of the Ozark region), many being employees of the state. The remainder came from scattered locations all over the country, especially large cities from which industrial plants had moved. Most retirees came from either the Midwest, especially Iowa and the Chicago area in Illinois (corresponding with a major source area of tourists to the Ozarks), or California. The latter were typically return migrants, having moved to the West Coast decades ago as a part of the important Ozark out-migration stream to the coast. The migration field of other migrants had no distinctive pattern, but had greater representation from the neighboring states of Missouri, Kansas, Oklahoma, and Texas. The economic opportunities in Harrison had become generally known in these areas.

In sum, the three types of migrants display different previous levels of knowledge of the destination area, have different types of search spaces, and of course chose Harrison for different reasons. The appearance of all three types of migrants at one destination is not atypical; many nonmetropolitan communities are growing as a result of the ability to attract a variety of migrants.

X. PROSPECT

Impacts of New Migration Patterns

Recent migration patterns are having impacts upon places of both origin and destination of migration streams. We will discuss some of these impacts upon: 1) central cities of metropolitan areas that continue to have large net out-migrations, 2) entire metropolitan systems within which population is gradually dispersing, and 3) small towns and rural areas that have recently experienced rapid growth through migration.

Central cities are losing migrants to virtually everywhere else—suburban and exurban places, as well as more distant metropolitan and nonmetropolitan places. Especially being depleted are middle- and upper-middle-income white populations. Attempts to retain people or attract them back have met with only little success. In most cities there are apartment districts that have retained or attracted young adults, singles or couples, who are in a stage of the life cycle when the attractions of city life outweigh the problems. Upon graduation to the family life cycle stage, however, a move to suburban environments is the rule. Similarly, many cities have districts in which upper-middle- and upper-income elderly or retired persons prefer apartment life in the city. Areas of historic or architectural significance have also attracted or retained people in various life cycle stages, but usually of relatively high income.

Efforts to keep persons of a wider range of incomes and life cycle stages include a few *urban homesteading* programs. They offer, at little or no cost, city or federally owned homes to people who are willing to live in them for a minimum time period and who will invest in the renewal of the home. Homesteading has had a modest start, is plagued with political problems, and has had little effect so far upon population movements within urban areas. Yet it has potential for reducing central city net out-migration.

The results of this net out-migration, coupled with the out-migration of business and industry, are that tax bases in central cities tend to decline. Yet they are still expected to provide various services to the people of the metropolitan area, including mass transportation and freeways, and cultural attractions such as museums and zoos. The resultant fiscal problems of many large and medium-sized central cities is one of the major urban problems of the 1970's.

We can observe further impacts by broadening our geographic perspective to entire metropolitan areas and neighboring exurban environments. As both people and activities (job and shopping, for example) disperse, the ability of mass transportation systems to serve the population adequately is reduced. A dependence upon the automobile has been intensifying, a trend which has important implications to society in general, including energy consumption. The concurrent lack of dispersal of minority and poor populations is causing many metropolitan areas to become dichotomized into contrasting populations in central cities versus suburbs. Continued efforts toward metropolitan unity in matters of schools, government, and transportation are strongly affected by this dichotomy.

Small towns, either in exurban regions or in more isolated locations, feel the effect of recent migration patterns, too. On the positive side, many people in such places have been dreaming of renewed growth and development for decades during which stagnation and net out-migration could not be avoided. "Growth" and its associated business opportunities were to many residents a dream—but when it comes, many small towns have difficulty coping with it. A sudden influx of migrants may necessitate major expansions of municipal services for which money may not be available. Also, there can be conflicts between long-time residents and newcomers who want to become a part of the community decision-making structure. Rapid need for change, coupled with a desire of newcomers with "different" ideas to participate in the change, can have important impacts, especially upon very small communities.

What Will Future Migration Patterns Be?

Will the migration trends of the 1970's continue into the 1980's? Will there be significant new migration streams that we cannot anticipate at this time? To address these questions, we will go back to the basic decision-making process and consider, in turn, the probable trends in decisions to move and in locational choices.

How will decisions to move change in the 1980's? We know that the numbers of persons in the over sixty-five age cohort, and even more the numbers of persons in retirement, will increase rapidly in the 1980's. Hence the number of persons "free" to move will increase and their ability and desire to make that decision will not likely diminish. This is because costs of living will always be important to persons on fixed incomes and migration is one of the ways to reduce those costs. Also the perceived problems of urban areas are not likely to diminish, meaning that the "push" of metropolitan areas will still affect retirees, and the "pull" of small towns and rural living should remain an important locational preference.

These perceived pushes and pulls are also likely to affect many persons in other life cycle stages. They may increasingly apply to suburban areas in addition to central cities, as awareness of problems in suburban areas emerges. In sum, there is reason to believe that there will be a continuation, and perhaps an increase, of many of the types of decisions to move that characterized the early 1970's. Major changes in the economy might modify the migration tendencies of persons whose decision-making is tied to business and industry—such changes are more likely to affect the decision where to move.

Where will people be migrating in the 1980's? Surely the major streams between metropolitan areas will continue, as the majority of the population and economic activities will be contained therein (although more dispersed within). But the dispersal of industry to places outside of metropolitan influence may or may not continue at the same rate. Some attribute this dispersal to the downturn of the economy in the early 1970's— whether or not a change in the economy will slow down the dispersal is debatable, but there is not likely to be a reversal to concentration partly because gradual dispersal of the population has meant dispersal of markets to which industry and business are closely tied. Moreover, industrial decision-makers are not likely to reverse their use of personal preferences or amenity locations for many types of plants. But this dispersal will remain gradual and the ties to metropolitan areas or their peripheries for a majority of migrant locational decisions are likely to continue.

Unless there are severe gasoline shortages and/or major price increases, the population is likely to continue its wandering ways for vacations as leisure time increases. Thus, the attractions of amenity/recreation areas for job seekers, retirees, and persons wanting to establish businesses should continue. The convergence of vacation spatial patterns and migration spatial patterns will not reverse itself.

This all argues for an extension through the 1980's of roughly the same migration patterns of the 1970's. What possible new or markedly changing migration streams might occur? First, there are rapidly increasing numbers of nonmetropolitan-born persons (especially Southern-born) reaching retirement age in major metropolitan areas, products of the great urban-bound migrations of the thirties, forties, and fifties. Some have retirement incomes that are adequate enough to make it possible for them to move. Because of their family and friendship ties, they are likely to decide to move "back home." Return migration, then, may dramatically increase, both to nonmetropolitan areas already experiencing some growth and to areas that are still experiencing net out-migration. This should include migration of whites to many nonmetropolitan areas and of blacks to the South.

Secondly, migration streams may be a function of institutional decisions. In a society with a continuing large governmental employment sector, the location decisions for major federal employment installations, military and otherwise, will have important impacts upon overall migration patterns. The decisions may be at the whims of pork-barrel legislators or other government decision-making structures which have had little concern as yet for impacts upon population distribution. Hence, they will be hard to predict. One trend could be a modest decline in major state university towns as prime attractors of migrants, since their greatest period of growth may be at an end.

Overall, the signs point to a general continuation of the patterns established in the 1960's and very observable in the early 1970's, trends which are consistent with recent population movements in other developed countries of the world. There should be continued preference for nonmetropolitan places, and the ability to act upon those preferences will quite likely increase.

BIBLIOGRAPHY

References Cited

Abler, Ronald, John S. Adams, and Peter Gould, 1971, *Spatial Organization,* Englewood Cliffs, N.J.: Prentice-Hall.

Adams, John S., 1969, "Directional Bias in Intra-Urban Migration," *Economic Geography,* Vol. 45, pp. 302-323.

Alonso, William, 1972, *Policy Implications of Inter-metropolitan Migration Flows,* Berkeley, Calif.: University of California, Institute of Urban and Regional Development, Working Paper No. 177.

Beale, Calvin L., 1975, *The Revival of Population Growth in Nonmetropolitan America,* Washington, D.C.: U.S. Department of Agriculture, Economic Research Service, ERS-605.

Beale, Calvin L., and Glenn V. Fuguitt, 1975, *The New Pattern of Nonmetropolitan Population Change,* Madison, Wisc.: University of Wisconsin, Center for Demography and Ecology, CDE Working Paper 75-22.

Bowles, Gladys K., Calvin L. Beale, and Everett S. Lee, 1975, *Net Migration of the Population, 1960-70, by Age, Sex, and Color,* Part 1—Northeastern States and Part 5—West South Central States, Athens, Ga.: University of Georgia Printing Department.

Brown, Lawrence A., and Eric G. Moore, 1970, "The Intra-Urban Migration Process: A Perspective," *Geografiska Annaler,* Vol. 52B, pp. 1-13.

Brown, Lawrence A., and John Holmes, 1971, "Search Behavior in an Intra-urban Migration Context: A Spatial Perspective," *Environment and Planning,* Vol. 3, pp. 307-326.

Ford, Larry, 1971, "Geographic Factors in the Origin, Evolution, and Diffusion of Rock and Roll Music," *Journal of Geography,* Vol. 70, pp. 455-464.

Francaviglia, Richard V., 1973, "Diffusion and Popular Culture," in David A. Lanegran and Risa Palm (eds.), *An Invitation to Geography,* New York: McGraw-Hill.

Fuguitt, Glenn V., and James J. Zuiches, 1975, "Residential Preferences and Population Distribution," *Demography,* Vol. 12, pp. 491-504.

Getis, Arthur, 1969, "Residential Location and the Journey from Work," *Proceedings,* Association of American Geographers, Vol. 1, pp. 55-59.

Gould, Peter R., 1969, *Spatial Diffusion,* Washington, D.C.: Association of American Geographers, Commission on College Geography, Resource Paper No. 4.

Gould, Peter, and Rodney White, 1974, *Mental Maps,* Harmondsworth, Middlesex: Penguin.

Groop, Richard E., 1976, *Small Town Population Change in Kansas—1950 to 1970,* unpublished Ph.D. dissertation, University of Kansas.

Henri, Florette, 1975, *Black Migration: Movement North, 1900-1920,* Garden City, N.Y.: Anchor Press/Doubleday.

Hirschberg, David, 1971, "The Social Security Administration's One-Percent Sample Data," in A. L. Ferris and E. S. Lee (eds.), *Research and the 1970 Census,* Oak Ridge, Tenn.: Southern Regional Demographic Group.

Holmes, John H., 1972, "Linkages Between External Commuting and Out-migration: Evidence from Middle-eastern Pennsylvania," *Economic Geography,* Vol. 48, pp. 406-420.

Lansing, John B., and Eva Mueller, 1967, *The Geographic Mobility of Labor,* Ann Arbor: University of Michigan, Institute for Social Research, Survey Research Center.

Lee, Everett S., 1966, "A Theory of Migration," *Demography,* Vol. 3, pp. 47-57.

Lewis, George K., 1972, "Population Change in Northern New England," *Annals of the Association of American Geographers,* Vol. 62, pp. 307-322.

Lloyd, Robert E., 1976, "Cognition, Preference, and Behavior in Space: An Examination of the Structural Linkages," *Economic Geography,* Vol. 241-253.

Long, Larry H., and Kristin A. Hansen, 1975, "Trends in Return Migration to the South," *Demography,* Vol. 12, pp. 601-614.

Lowry, Ira S., 1966, *Migration and Metropolitan Growth: Two Analytical Models,* San Francisco: Chandler.

Morrison, Peter A., 1971, *The Propensity to Move: A Longitudinal Analysis,* Santa Monica, Calif.: Rand Paper No. R-654-HUD.

Morrison, Peter A., and Judith P. Wheeler, 1976, "Rural Renaissance in America? The Revival of Population Growth in Remote Areas," *Population Bulletin,* Vol. 31, Washington, D.C.: Population Reference Bureau.

Muller, Peter O., 1976, *The Outer City: Geographical Consequences of the Urbanization of the Suburbs,* Washington, D.C.: Association of American Geographers, Resource Paper No. 75-2.

Palm, Risa, 1976, "Real Estate Agents and Geographical Information," *Geographical Review,* Vol. 66, pp. 266-280.

Renshaw, Vernon, 1974, "Using Gross Migration Data Compiled from the Social Security Sample File, *Demography,* Vol. 11, pp. 143-148.

Roseman, Curtis C., 1971a, "Channelization of Migration Flows from the Rural South to the Industrial Midwest," *Proceedings,* Association of American Geographers, Vol. 3, pp. 140-146.

———, 1971b, "Migration as a Spatial and Temporal Process," *Annals of the Association of American Geographers,* Vol. 61, pp. 589-598.

———, 1976, "Migration of Whites to Central Cities and Quality of Life," *Geographical Survey,* Vol. 5, pp. 14-21.

Sly, David F., 1974, "Tourism's Role in Migration to Florida: Basic Tourist-Migration Relationship," *Governmental Research Bulletin,* The Florida State University, Institute for Social Research, Vol. 11.

Stouffer, Samuel A., 1940, "Intervening Opportunities: A Theory Relating Mobility and Distance," *American Sociological Review,* Vol. 5, pp. 845-867.

———, 1960, "Intervening Opportunities and Competing Migrants," *Journal of Regional Science,* Vol. 2, pp. 1-26.

Stutz, Frederick P., 1977, *Social Aspects of Interaction and Transportation,* Washington, D.C.: Association of American Geographers, Resource Paper No. 76-2.

Sundquist, James L., 1975, *Dispersing Population: What America Can Learn From Europe,* Washington, D.C.: The Brookings Institution.

Svart, Larry M., 1976, "Environmental Preference Migration: A Review," *Geographical Review,* Vol. 66, pp. 314-330.

Thompson, Derek, 1974, "Spatial Interaction Data," *Annals*

of the Association of American Geographers, Vol. 64, pp. 560-575.

Tilly, Charles, 1968, "Race and Migration to the American City," Chapter 5 in James Q. Wilson (ed.) *The Metropolitan Enigma,* Cambridge, Mass.: Harvard University Press.

Trott, Charles E., 1971, "An Analysis of Outmigration," *Proceedings,* Business and Economics Statistics Section, American Statistical Association, pp. 192-200.

U.S. Bureau of the Census, 1967, *Census of Population 1960, Migration Between State Economic Areas,* Washington, D.C.: U.S. Government Printing Office, Report PC(2)-2E.

———, 1971, *Statistical Abstract of the United States: 1971,* 92nd Edition, Washington, D.C.: U.S. Government Printing Office.

———, 1972, *Census of Population 1970, Migration Between State Economic Areas,* Washington, D.C.: U.S. Government Printing Office, Report PC(2)-2E.

———, 1973, *Census of Population 1970, Detailed Characteristics,* Washington, D.C.: U.S. Government Printing Office, Final Report PC(1)-D1, United States Summary.

———, 1975a, *Current Population Reports, Population Estimates,* Washington, D.C.: U.S. Government Printing Office, Series P-25 and P-26 (various numbers).

———, 1975b, *Current Population Reports, Mobility of the Population of the United States: March 1970 to March 1975,* Washington, D.C.: U.S. Government Printing Office, Series P-20, No. 285.

———, 1976, *Current Population Reports, Population Profile of the United States: 1975,* Washington, D.C.: U.S. Government Printing Office, Series P-20, No. 292.

U.S. Social Security Administration, 1971, *Basic Statistical Data Files Available to Outside Researchers,* Washington, D.C.: Department of Health, Education and Welfare, Social Security Administration, Office of Research and Statistics.

Vining, Daniel R., Jr., and Thomas R. Kontuly, 1976, "Interregional Population Dispersal," unpublished paper, University of Pennsylvania, Department of Regional Science.

Wolpert, Julian, 1965, "Behavioral Aspects of the Decision to Migrate," *Papers and Proceedings,* Regional Science Association, Vol. 15, pp. 159-172.

Further Reading

Adams, Russell, B., 1969, "U.S. Metropolitan Migration: Dimensions and Predictability," *Proceedings,* Association of American Geographers, Vol. 1, pp. 1-6.

Beale, Calvin L., 1974, "Rural Development: Population and Settlement Prospects," *Journal of Soil and Water Conservation,* Vol. 29, pp. 23-27.

Berry, Brian J. L., 1970, "The Geography of the United States in the Year 2000," *Ekistics,* Vol. 29, pp. 339-351.

———, 1976, "The Counterurbanization Process: Urban America Since 1970," in Brian J. L. Berry (ed.), *Urbanization and Counterurbanization,* Volume 11, Urban Affairs Annual Reviews, Beverly Hills, Calif.: Sage.

Berry, Brian J. L., and Q. Gillard, 1976, *The Changing Shape of Metropolitan America: Commuting Patterns, Urban Fields and Decentralization Processes, 1960-70,* Cambridge, Mass.: Ballinger.

Boorstin, David, 1975, "Rural Migration," *Editorial Research Reports,* Vol. II, pp. 583-600.

Brown, David L., 1975, *Socioeconomic Characteristics of Growing and Declining Nonmetropolitan Counties,* Washington, D.C.: U.S. Department of Agriculture, Economic Research Service, AER-306.

Brown, Lawrence A., Susan O. Gustavus, and Edward J.

Malecki, 1977, "Awareness Space Characteristics in a Migration Context," *Environment and Behavior* (forthcoming).

DeJong, Gordon, F., 1975, "Population Redistribution Policies: Alternatives from the Netherlands, Great Britain, and Israel," *Social Science Quarterly,* Vol. 56, pp. 262-273.

DeJong, Gordon F., and Ralph R. Sell, 1975, *Residential Preferences and Migration Behavior,* report submitted to the Center for Population Research, National Institutes of Health, Department of Health, Education, and Welfare, University Park, Pa.: The Pennsylvania State University.

Delaney, Paul, 1974, "Shift to Exurbia Continuing in U.S.," *New York Times,* April 7, p. 40.

Egan, Richard, 1975, "How Ya Gonna Keep 'Em in Metropolis," *The National Observer,* May 31, p. 3.

Eloridge, Hope T., 1965, "Primary, Secondary, and Return Migration in the United States, 1955-60," *Demography,* Vol. 2, pp. 444-462.

Fuguitt, Glenn V., 1971, "The Places Left Behind: Population Trends and Policy for Rural America," *Rural Sociology,* Vol. 36, pp. 459-470.

Goldstein, Sidney, 1976, "Facets of Redistribution: Research Challenges and Opportunities," *Demography,* Vol. 13, pp. 423-434.

———, 1954, "Repeated Migration as a Factor in High Mobility Rates," *American Sociological Review,* Vol. 19, pp. 536-541.

Goodrich, Carter, 1936, *Migration and Economic Opportunity,* Philadelphia: University of Pennsylvania Press.

Green, Bernal L., Lloyd D. Bender, and Rex R. Campbell, 1970, *Migration into Four Communities in the Ozarks Region,* Fayetteville, Ark.: Arkansas Agricultural Experiment Station Bulletin 756.

Gustavus, Susan O., and Lawrence A. Brown, 1977, "Place Attributes in a Migration Decision Context," *Environment and Planning* (forthcoming).

Hacker, David W., 1974, "Back to the Boonies," *National Observer,* January 5, p. 1.

Haenszel, William, 1967, "Concept, Measurement and Data in Migration Analysis," *Demography,* Vol. 4, pp. 253-261.

Hagerstrand, Torsten, 1957, "Migration and Area," in D. Hannergerg *et al.* (eds.), *Migration in Sweden,* Lund Studies in Geography No. 13B, Lund: Gleerup.

Hansen, Niles M., 1973, *The Future of Nonmetropolitan America,* Lexington, Mass.: Lexington.

Humphrey, Craig R., and Ralph R. Sell, 1975, "The Impact of Controlled Access Highways on Population Growth in Pennsylvanian Nonmetropolitan Communities, 1940-1970," *Rural Sociology,* Vol. 40, pp. 332-343.

Immel, A. Richard, 1974, "Try as They Might, the Residents of Oregon Can't Deter New Residents," *Wall Street Journal,* May 22, p. 17.

Kau, James B., and C. F. Sirmans, 1976, "New, Repeat, and Return Migration: A Study of Migrant Types," *Southern Economic Journal,* Vol. 43, pp. 1144-1148.

Kirschenbaum, Alan, 1971, "Patterns of Migration from Metropolitan to Nonmetropolitan Areas: Changing Ecological Factors Affecting Family Mobility," *Rural Sociology,* Vol. 36, pp. 315-325.

Lamb, Richard, 1975, *Metropolitan Impacts on Rural America,* Chicago: University of Chicago, Department of Geography, Research Paper No. 162.

Leslie, Gerald R., and Arthur H. Richardson, 1961, "Lifecycle, Career Pattern, and the Decision to Move," *American Sociological Review,* Vol. 26, pp. 894-902.

Lloyd, Robert E., 1977, "Consumer Behavior After Migration: A Reassessment Process," *Economic Geography,* Vol. 53, pp. 14-27.

MacDonald, John S., and Leatrice D. MacDonald, 1964,

"Chain Migration, Ethnic Neighborhood Formation and Social Networks," *Milbank Memorial Fund Quarterly,* Vol. 42, pp. 82-97.

Mangalam, J. J., 1968, *Human Migration. A Guide to Migration Literature in English 1955-1962,* Lexington, Ky.: University of Kentucky Press.

Morgan, David J., 1977, *Patterns of Population Distribution: A Residential Preference Model and its Dynamic,* Chicago: University of Chicago, Department of Geography, Research Paper No. 176 (forthcoming).

Morgan, David J., and James R. Murray, 1974, *Determinants and Effects of Expressed Preferences for Residential Location,* Chicago: National Opinion Research Center.

Morrison, Peter A., 1977, "Migration and Access: New Public Concerns of the 1970s," paper presented at the annual meeting of the American Association for the Advancement of Science, Denver, Colo.

————, 1971, "Chronic Movers and the Future Redistribution of Population: A Longitudinal Analysis," *Demography,* Vol. 8, pp. 171-184.

————, 1975, *The Current Demographic Context of National Growth and Development,* Santa Monica, Calif.: Rand Paper No. P-5514.

Myers, George C., Robert McGinnis, and George Masnik, 1967, "The Duration of Residence Approach to a Dynamic Model of Internal Migration: The Axiom of Cumulative Inertia," *Eugenics Quarterly,* Vol. 14, pp. 121-126.

Nordheimer, Jon, 1976, "Sunbelt Leads Nation in Growth of Population," *New York Times,* Feb. 8, p. 1.

Ragatz, Richard Lee, 1970, "Vacation Homes in the Northeastern United States: Seasonality in Population Distribution," *Annals of the Association of American Geographers,* Vol. 60, pp. 447-455.

Reed, Roy, 1975, "Influx of Arkansas People a Mixed Blessing," *New York Times,* May 19, p. 18.

Reinhold, Robert, 1976, "More Elderly Retiring in North," *New York Times,* Feb. 1, p. 1.

Roseman, Curtis C., 1975, "Population Redistribution in the United States and in Illinois," *Illinois Business Review,* Vol. 32, No. 8, pp. 6-8.

Rossi, Peter H., 1955, *Why Families Move: A Study in the Social Psychology of Urban Residential Mobility,* Glencoe, Ill: The Free Press.

Schnell, George A., and Mark S. Monmonier, 1976, "U.S. Population Change 1960-70: Simplification, Meaning, and Mapping," *Journal of Geography,* Vol. 75, pp. 280-291.

Schwind, Paul J., 1975, "A General Field Theory of Migration: United States, 1955-60," *Economic Geography,* Vol. 51, pp. 1-16.

Serow, William J., Julia H. Martin, and Michael A. Spar, 1974, "Migration Between State Economic Areas: Review of the Data and Some Initial Analyses," *Review of Public Data Use,* Vol. 2, pp. 1-9.

Shaw, Paul R., 1975, *Migration Theory and Fact, A Review and Bibliography of Current Literature,* Philadelphia: Regional Science Research Institute, Bibliography Series No. 5.

Shyrock, Henry S., 1964, *Population Mobility Within the United States,* Chicago: University of Chicago Community and Family Center.

Simmons, James W., 1968, "Changing Residence in the City," *Geographical Review,* Vol. 58, pp. 622-651.

Speare, Alden, Jr., Sidney Goldstein, and William H. Frey, 1974, *Residential Mobility, Migration, and Metropolitan Change,* Cambridge, Mass.: Ballinger.

Sterba, James P., 1976, "Houston, as Energy Capital, Sets Pace in Sunbelt Boom," *New York Times,* Feb. 10, p. 1.

Taeuber, Karl E., L. Chiazze, Jr., and W. Haenszel, 1968, *Migration in the United States: An Analysis of Residence Histories,* Public Health Monograph No. 77, Public Health Service, U.S. Department of Health, Education and Welfare, Washington, D.C.: U.S. Government Printing Office.

Tarver, James D., 1972, "Patterns of Population Change Among Southern Non-metropolitan Towns, 1950-1970," *Rural Sociology,* Vol. 37, pp. 53-72.

Time, 1976, "Americans on the Move," March 15, pp. 54-64.

Tucker, C. Jack, 1976, "Changing Patterns of Migration Between Metropolitan and Nonmetropolitan Areas in the United States: Recent Evidence," *Demography,* Vol. 13, pp. 435-443.

U.S. Commission on Population Growth and the American Future, 1972, *Population Distribution and Policy,* Sara Mills Mazie (ed.), Vol. V of Commission Research Reports, Washington, D.C.: U.S. Government Printing Office.

U.S. Department of Agriculture, 1963, *A Place to Live,* The Yearbook of Agriculture 1963, Washington, D.C.: U.S. Government Printing Office.

U.S. News and World Report, 1975, "Okies of the 70's—Mass Migration in Search of Jobs," March 24, p. 16.

————, 1975, "Out of the Cities, Back to the Country," March 31, p. 46.

Uhlenberg, Peter, 1973, "Noneconomic Determinants of Nonmigration: Sociological Considerations for Migration Theory," *Rural Sociology,* Vol. 38, pp. 296-311.

Ullman, Edward L., 1954, "Amenities as a Factor in Regional Growth," *Geographical Review,* Vol. 44, pp. 119-132.

Vanderkamp, John, 1972, "Return Migration: Its Significance and Behavior," *Western Economic Journal,* Vol. 10, pp. 460-465.

Wardwell, John M., 1977, "Equilibrium and Change in Nonmetropolitan Growth," *Rural Sociology* (forthcoming).

Wolpert, Julian, 1967, "Distance and Directional Bias in Inter-urban Migratory Streams," *Annals of the Association of American Geographers,* Vol. 57, pp. 605-616.

Zelinsky, Wilbur, 1971, "The Hypothesis of the Mobility Transition," *Geographical Review,* Vol. 61, pp. 219-249.

————, 1975, "Nonmetropolitan Pennsylvania: A Demographic Revolution in the Making?" *Earth and Mineral Sciences,* Vol. 45, No. 1, pp. 1-4.

Zelinsky, Wilbur *et al.,* 1974, *Population Change and Redistribution in Non-metropolitan Pennsylvania, 1940-1970,* report submitted to the Center for Population Research, National Institutes of Health, Department of Health, Education, and Welfare, University Park, Pa.: The Pennsylvania State University.

Zuiches, James J., and David L. Brown, 1977, "The Changing Character of the Nonmetropolitan Population, 1950-1975," in Thomas R. Ford (ed.), *Rural Society in the United States—Current Trends and Issues,* Ames, Ia: Iowa State University Press (forthcoming)

Consulting Services Publications
available from

Association of American Geographers
1710 Sixteenth St., N.W.
Washington, D.C. 20009

Geography as a Discipline, R. Huke, V. Malmstrom, 1973
Sources of Funds for College Geography Departments. S. J. Natoli, 1973
Planning College Geography Facilities: Guidelines for Space and Equipment (CCG General Series Publication No. 12), R. H. Stoddard, 1973
Community Internships for Undergraduate Geography Students, K. E. Corey, A. W. Stuart, 1973
Undergraduate Program Development in Geography, T. Burke, 1973
Geography in the Two-Year Colleges (CCG General Series Publication No. 10), Panel on Geography in the Two-Year Colleges, 1970

Association of American Geographers
1710 Sixteenth St., N.W.
Washington, D.C. 20009

Nonprofit Org.
U.S. Postage
PAID
Permit #930
Richmond, Va.

1174